The Modern Olympics

Between Nationalism and the Migration Movement

Maria Schüler

Bibliographic information published by the German National Library:

The German National Library lists this publication in the National Bibliography; detailed bibliographic data are available on the Internet at http://dnb.dnb.de.

ISBN: 9783961169658
This book is also available as an ebook.

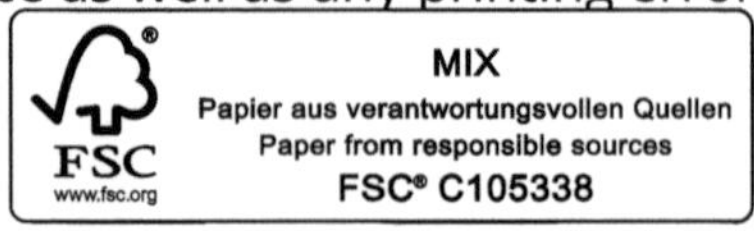

Throughout history, the number of participating countries at the Olympic Games has grown (Figure 5). Only in 1978 and 1980, compared to the previous and following Games, the number of countries decreased significantly. With the increasing number of participant countries, the notoriety of the Olympic Games also extended. As a result, the number of partners in the OCOGs (Organising Committees for the Olympic Games) sponsorship programs increased (Figure 1). In 2018, there were more partners than ever before. Through investment in the Olympic Games, sponsors obtain many advantages. On the one hand, through advertisement their notoriety increases. On the other hand, the international cross-linking of sponsors extends. With the growing international fame, every time the Olympic Games are held, a certain motto that refers to international links is represented. In Rio 2016, the Olympic Games caused a sensation with the establishment of a Refugee Olympic Team (ROT). During the presentation of the idea behind the foundation of the Refugee Olympic Team, the former president of the IOC (International Olympic Committee), Thomas Bach, declared:

> This will be a symbol of hope for all the refugees in our world, and will make the world better aware of the magnitude of the crisis. It is also a signal to the international community that refugees are our fellow human beings and are an enrichment to society. (IOC, 2016)

As a result, the debate of national representation and awareness grew extensively. People's positions towards the migration movement strongly differ from each other. Some people agree with the IOC's intention to support the migration movement and particular refugees. On the other hand, many people criticise the decreasing national character of the Olympic Games. However, at the Olympic Games in Rio 2016, the ROT marched between the Olympic flag and the Brazilian Olympic Team (cf. ibid). During the introduction of the ROT concept, Bach postulates:

> These refugees have no home, no team, no flag, no national anthem. We will offer them a home in the Olympic Village together with all the athletes of the word. The Olympic anthem will be played in their honour and the Olympic flag will lead them into the Olympic Stadium. This will be a symbol of hope for all the refugees in our world, and will make the world better aware of the magnitude of this crisis. It is also a signal to the international community that refugees are our fellow human beings and are an enrichment to society. These refugee athletes will show the world that despite the unimaginable tragedies that they have faced, anyone can contribute to society through their talent, skills and strength of the human spirit. (ibid)

In the context of the selection of the athletes of the ROT, the IOC cooperated with the NOCs (National Olympic Committees). 'NOCs around the world were asked to identify any refugee athlete with the potential to qualify for the Olympic Games Rio 2016.' (IOC, 2016). The criteria to which refugees must adhere to be selected are 'sporting level, official refugee status verified by the United Nations, and personal situation and background.' (ibid).

After the foundation of the ROT, people became more a more aware of the question of national representation in the Olympic Games. Since the first modern Olympics, foreign-born athletes have competed for other nations, but the establishment of the ROT – which does not represent any one specific nation – expanded debates over nationalism and national belonging. For this reason, this Bachelor Thesis will explore whether the Olympics strengthen nationalism or if they promote international movements. In reference to the increasing attention on migration, the specific perspective of foreign-born athletes will be focused on. Furthermore, this paper addresses the relationship between nationalism and internationalism. The analysis intends to explain nationalism in modern society and how nationalism affects, or gets affected by, cross-national movements. Through a closer look at the modern Olympic Games, the analysis will refer to global sport and the trade of foreign-born athletes. Moreover, the ideological, religious, economic and political character of the Olympic will be highlighted. Therefore, the aspects of ideology and religion will be considered as forms of belief systems, while economy and politics refer to rational thoughts and actions. It must be mentioned that economy and politics can also have religious and ideological features. Hence, the content of this Bachelor Thesis suggests that, in general, the fields are separated in analysis. After the exploration of each field, an analysis follows that puts all areas into one context. The analysis of this Bachelor Thesis is based on the following six assumptions:

1. In modern society, sport is only a tool of power division, with the Olympics as a practical example.

2. National awareness cannot be an important aspect of the Olympics, if nations trade with foreign-born athletes.

3. Nationalism and Internationalism need to be separated in theory but they are co-existing in practice.

4. In times of double citizenship and diasporas, nationalism is getting weaker.

5. The Olympics lost the connection to their religious roots and became a
global promotion for each countries' identity.

Moreover, in each context all terms used will be specifically interpreted in order to avoid general definitions. All outcomes or results of the analysis and conclusion is only an assumption come to using thematic exploration.

The second chapter (*2. Theoretical Perspectives of Migration*) explores theoretical approaches to the migration movement. At the beginning, different disciplines of migration theory are analysed. Furthermore, this chapter makes an attempt to combine particular disciplines with each other. According to this, the research fields of sociology, history, political sciences, and economics are focused on. In the chapter *2.2. Internationalism and Transnationalism,* the concept of international and transnational theories are explored. Moreover, global relations and cross-national systems are units of this analysis. For the first time, in this chapter, the terms 'state', 'nation', and 'nationalism' are explored in the context of trans- and international theories. The following chapter (*2.3. Economic and Political Approaches*) explains the world-systems theory and the human capital theory. As two dominant approaches of modern society, these two theories connect the economic and political character on a global level. These theories are insofar important for the central analysis, as hypotheses 1 and 5 suggest a growing rationalisation and industrialisation of modern society and global sport. Moreover, nations and states are put into an international context and are considered as agents in transnational relations. Chapter *2.4. Communities and Social Actions* compares Weber's four types of actions with Durkheim's approaches of analysing the religious character of society. In chapter 3. *The Ideological Character of Nationalism,* theoretical approaches of ideology analysis are considered, as well as an analysis of nationalism as a form of ideology. The chapter *3.2. State and Nation* explores conceptual understandings of 'state' and 'nation', as well as 'nation-state'. These terms are not only theoretically compared, but their historical background is also considered. Furthermore, the relation to previous chapters' contents, such as political and economic perspectives and communities, are included in the analysis of nation and state. Chapter *3.2.2. Citizenship* addresses interpretations of social membership. The conceptual understanding of citizenship is analysed. Furthermore, national-belonging, double citizenship, loyalty, sovereignty and migration are unit of the analysis. Moreover, the political and legal aspect is considered. Focus of the chapter *3.3. Nationalism* is nationalism theory. Traditional and modern concepts of nationalism are introduced, as well as aspects like national identity, citizenship, and migration. As a phenomenon, in *3.3.3. Diaspora and Diaspora Theory*, a particular form of nationalism and identity is focused on. Aspects of solidarity, national awareness, and migration are considered. The chapter *4.1. Sport and Sporting Capital* analyses modern sport in the context of human capital theory, embedded in the world-system. Furthermore, the Olympic Movement is embedded in previous theoretical outcomes. In *4.2.1. Historical Impacts – The Ancient Olympics,* the origins of the modern Olympics are focused on. In the 2nd subchapter of *4.2. The Modern Olympic Movement,* the IOC is considered. Moreover, Pierre de Coubertin, former president of the IOC, and his idea of Olympism is introduced. The 3rd subchapter analysis the religious character of the Olympics. In *5. Analysis and Evaluation,* all results and outcomes of previous chapters are considered and related with each other. Furthermore, statistics and data of financial efforts and migration researches of the Olympics are analysed. The following subchapter (*5.3. Changing Nationality*) contains an analysis of the concept of nationality switching among foreign-born athletes. Political and economic aspects, as well as national awareness, are referred to. The chapter *5.4. Nationalism or Internationalism?* explores the central question of this paper. In this chapter, previous analysis results are considered and put into one context. The last chapter of this Bachelor Thesis represents results of the analysis and the introduced theories and approaches. Furthermore, the hypotheses are answered and a final review is presented. Moreover, assumptions of future analyses are made.

Migration is a societal phenomenon. Debates about migration are varied and extend over multiple fields of society. Politics, economy, and sociology are just some examples. The previous fields of analysis are the main perspectives that this Bachelor Thesis explores. This chapter explores the different disciplines of migration theory and the relation between them. Furthermore, the trans- and international approaches are considered in particular. Subsequently, the dominant approaches of world-systems and human capital theory are analysed. The analysing unit of the first named theory are global and international dynamics. In general, this approach is focused on political incidents and reciprocal effects within political relations. Human capital theory is analysed as a particular part of the world-system. Hence, this Bachelor Thesis considers human capital theory as embedded approach in world-systems theory. In addition, the connection of political and economic field is considered. In relation to the subject matter of this Bachelor Thesis, migration is examined as specific form of human capital.

2.1. General Migration Theory

Nowadays, there are plenty of research disciplines in migration theory. Each discipline has manifold analytical approaches, in which specific concepts exist. Unfortunately, analysis rarely combines these disciplines. Therefore, theoretical concepts and core assumptions are rarely shared between disciplines (cf. Brettell & Hollifield, 2015, p. 2). We can roughly categorise the following disciplines: law, economics, demography, history, sociology, political sciences, anthropology and geography (cf. ibid, p. 4). In an attempt to define these disciplines, the ideas of Brettell and Hollifield gives a plausible explanation. In their book *Migration Theory. Talking Across Disciplines* they categorise four fields of analysis. They separate the following research areas: the research question, the level or unit of analysis, dominant theories of the discipline and a sample hypothesis (cf. ibid). For this Bachelor Thesis, the of disciplines of economics, political sciences, history and sociology are important to explore. In economics, the research question focuses on the explanation of propensity of migration and the effects it leads to. Hence, the analysing field is on a micro-level. Economic theories primarily pay attention to utility maximisation and cost benefits. Therefore, the hypothesis concerns itself with the human capital of migrants. Political sciences question states' difficulty in controlling migration. Here, the field of the research question is on a macro-level. The units of analysis are international and political systems. In political sciences, the dominant theories concentrate on rationalisation and institutionalisation. Brettell and Hollifield consider the sample hypothesis that states are generally captured by immigrant interests. Historical research concentrates on changes in relations and phenomena over a long time. For this reason, the level of analysis varies spatially and temporally. Because of a long-lasting analysis, the dominant theory is based on periodisation. In historical research, Brettell and Hollifield refuse to give a sample hypothesis. They argue that there is no hypothesis which could be applied over many periods. Sociological migration research tries to discover reasons for exclusion and incorporation. On a micro-level, the subject of analysis is social classes and ethnic groups. The principal theories of sociology are structuralism and institutionalism. The sample hypothesis that Brettell and Hollifield mention assumes that incorporation changes with human and social capital. Via rational theories, economists try to explain human behaviour and, similarly to sociologists, they focus on selectivity as an important factor of migration (cf. Brettell & Hollifield, 2015, p. 7). The macro-economic question of migration is 'what immigrants add to the economy of the receiving society [...] [and] what emigrants take away from the economy of the sending society' (ibid, p. 8). Therefore, migrants are analysed as utility maximisers in connection to cost-benefit conditions. The analysis of cost-benefits and push-pull factors are closely connected to neoclassical economy (cf. Hollifield & Wong, 2015, p. 228). In political sciences, three main subject that are central to the analysis exist, which are often analytically separated. The first one is 'the role of nation-state in controlling migration flows and hence its borders' (Brettell & Hollifield, 2015, p. 9); the second one is 'the impact of migration on the institutions of sovereignty and citizenship' (ibid); and the third one 'the question of incorporations' (ibid). In migration, scientific political approaches also focus on rational choice actions. Hence, the analysing unit can also be on a micro-level: the interest-based level. Alternatively, some political scientists prefer to explore 'institutional, historical, and/or constructivist explanations for migration, immigration incorporation, participation, and citizenship in the advanced industrial democracy' (ibid). Historical assumptions are applicable to 'more groups (or individuals) at a particular place and time, but they can also be applied over the long durations of time in the area of migration history.' (ibid, p. 5). Contrary to economists, historians 'may not engage directly in the development of theoretical models that predict behaviour' (ibid, p. 5). Equally to social scientists, they focus more on theory to elaborate their questions and analyse their arguments (cf. ibid). In migration, sociologist try to find an explanation for the occurrence of migration and also who tends to migrate. They focus on the issues of selectivity (cf. Brettell & Hollifield, 2015, p. 6). For example, many debates exist about the extent of 'positive selections' of migrants in the educational field (cf. FitzGerald, 2015, p. 120). Selectivity is defined as follows:

> *A process that determines whether certain types of individuals are more likely to migrate than others from the same sending region, whether as part of regulated recruitment or via self-selection.* (Bartram, et al., 2014, p. 128; italics in the original)

In addition to the first subject of political sciences and the selectivity subject of sociology, the analysis of political sociologists is also relevant. Its focus is 'the role of states in shaping migration flows.' (FitzGerald, 2015, p. 121). At this point, FitzGerald gives the example of the political decision of the Canadian government in the period of World War II, when Canada accepted Polish refugees 'on the condition that they work in agriculture for two years' (ibid p. 124). Even nowadays, Canada desires immigrants only up to a specific point. Therefore, the chances of admission of individuals are higher if they are well-educated and young (cf. Bartram, et al., 2014, p. 5). This suggests that authority, power, control, and influence are the basic levels of politics (cf. Hollifield & Wong, 2015, p. 235). The main question in sociological analysis of migration is: 'How is migration sustained over time […]. And what happens once these population are settled' (Brettell & Hollifield, 2015, p. 6)? In sociology, the theoretical framework is quite similar to the one in anthropology. These two disciplines work closely together and influence the analysis of each other. Hence, transnationalism and network analysis are research fields of sociology and anthropology. These two research approaches are derived from world-systems analysis (cf. Hollifield & Wong, 2015, p. 229).

2.2. Internationalism and Transnationalism

'[I]nternational migration is the movement of people to another country, leading to temporary or permanent resettlement' (Bartram, et al., 2014, p. 4; italics in the original). This approach to international migration theory is specific to the field of the global movement. It does not focus on who migrates and how migrants are integrated into their destination country, but rather international migration theory is a macro-perspective on migration. Therefore, the core question is: What attracts potential migrants and what are reasons for their movement? The keys for international migration research are push- and

pull-factors. These factors are the basis for making any assumption about the emergence of migration flows, and their extent (cf. Bean & Brown, 2015, p. 69). Moreover, a global perspective on migration challenges includes the question of social membership and national identities (cf. Bartram, et al., 2014, p. 4). Hence, it is necessary to consider the term 'nation', because without a concept of the nation it will not be possible to analyse the inter*national* relation of migration (cf. ibid). It can be suggested that 'migration is simply part of the inexorable process of globalization over which states have little control.' (Hollifield & Wong, 2015, p. 245). The rise of free trade and the extent of international migration are closely connected with each other (cf. ibid). Therefore, migrants can be defined as goods of international economic traffic. The economic profit of migrants for nations in international free trade is a common assumption of international migration research.

> In looking at migration and international relations, we are concerned not just with domestic politics […] but with foreign policy, national security and identity, and the nature and structure of the international system. (ibid, p. 246)

As an analytical aspect of migration in international relations, the unit of analysis are states and international systems, instead of interest groups and individuals (cf. ibid). Hollifield and Wong categorise three schools of international relation research. The first school is realism or neorealism; the second, liberal institutionalism; and the third, transnationalism. In political realism, the basic assumption is that states are rational actors, and that their 'behaviour is constrained by the anarchic structure of the international system.' (ibid, p. 248). In the context of migration, two dominant hypotheses in political realism exist. The fist hypothesis assumes that 'states will open or close their borders when it is in their national interest' (ibid, p. 248). Hence, migration policy is seen as a matter of national identity and security (cf. ibid). The second hypothesis suggests migration policy to be 'a function of international systemic factors, namely, the distribution of power in the international system and the relative position of states.' (Hollifield & Wong, 2015, pp. 248-249). Inevitably, every theory has its weakness. In the case of realism, Hollifield and Wong state that it is politically overdetermined. Therefore, political realism is not able to explain the enduring extent of world migration (cf. ibid, p. 250). One assumption of the school of liberal institutionalism is that 'states are more willing to risk opening their economies to trade […] if there is some type of international regime […] that can regulate these flows' (cf., p. 256). Another assumption focuses on the maintenance of an open world economy. This maintenance strongly depends 'on coalitions of powerful interest in the most dominant, liberal states.' (Hollifield & Wong, 2015). In transnational theory, one approach is the weakening of nation-states by transnationalism itself. Subjects of transnational analysis are sovereignty and the management of power. These two units are the area in which a nation-state gets weakened by transnational movements (cf. ibid, p. 250). Contrary to realism, transnational analysis does not limit actors to nation-states. Hence, transnational studies 'bypass the regulatory authority of sovereign states.' (ibid). With the rise of transnational economies, transnational communities were also created. This was a result of the movement of workers from one country to another. Ever since, workers have been forced to migrate, otherwise they would risk their economic existence (cf. ibid, p. 251). The aim of transnational studies is to overcome territorialism and essentialism. Transnational theory refutes the assumption of a congruence of state, society and state territory (cf. Faist, et al., 2014, p. 27). One of the main problems that transnational studies needs to challenge is the reification of categories of national thinking, such as ethnicity and nation (cf. ibid). In addition to this, it is possible to identify three major methodological problems in transnational studies (cf. ibid, p. 154). The first methodological problem is the common assumption that the nation-state is the only relevant context in which empirical studies of international migration can be made in: the state is interpreted as a container. This is what can be called methodological nationalism (cf. ibid). As mentioned above, the problem results in the assumption of state and society as territorial congruence. Consequently, social sciences tend to analyse the nation-state as a natural political and social structure (cf. ibid). Martins describes the problem as follows:

> In general, macro-sociological work has largely submitted to national pre-definitions of social realities: a kind of methodological nationalism— which does not necessarily go together with political nationalism on the part of the researcher— imposes itself in practice with national community as the terminal unit and boundary condition for the demarcation of problems and phenomena for social science. (Martins, 2014, p. 276)

Therefore, in the context of migration studies, the problem of methodological nationalism is the assumption of national institutions as the dominant or general context of migration analysis (cf. Faist, et. al., 2014, p. 155). The second major methodological problem of transnational studies is that nationality and ethnicity are often not questioned, and are seen as the dominant context of characterising agents. As a result, national and ethnic membership are naturalised (cf. ibid, p. 154). This approach is called essentialism. The emerging problem is the homogenisation of groups. This analysis disregards the heterogeneity of migrant categories, and creates a general ethnic and national perspective which resembles methodological nationalism (cf. Faist, et. al., 2014, p. 154). The last major methodological problem of transnational studies is the question of the perspective of researchers. Their positionality gets questioned (cf. ibid, p. 155). For example, the distribution of subsidies or the interpretation of socio-scientific concepts can have impacts on the perspective of researchers. A specific form of transnational theory regards the role of diasporas. Diaspora theories have emerged in recent decades as a new way of analysing transnationalism, and transnational communities (cf. Castles, et al., 2014, p. 41). The reason for this is the 'increased the ability of migrants to foster multiple identities' (ibid). In a later chapter of this Bachelor Thesis, the phenomenon of diaspora theories is explained in detail.

2.3. Economic and Political Approaches

World-systems theory is a dominant approach of the analysis of global relations. This chapter considers the development and origins of this theory. Furthermore, key elements of world-systems theory are analysed. Territorial factors, nations as agents, and capitalistic aspects are specifically focused on. Afterwards, the origins of human capital theory are explored. This theory considers cost-benefit approaches in migration. Education, as a particular form human capital is outlined. Physical education is especially important to identify as a theme of this Bachelor Thesis to create connections with the later central analysis.

2.3.1. World-Systems Theory

In the nineteenth century, world-systems theory originated as a result of the 'rejection of social science categories' (Wallerstein, 2013, p. 1). The theory 'was a protest or resistance movement within the structures of knowledge' (Lee, 2011, p. 27). Inevitably, the growing structures of knowledge led to a 'process of rationalizing', and this turned into a crisis. A result of this process is a changing world view from an autonomous unit towards a relational system (cf. ibid, p. 36). According to Lee, this rationalisation can also be called 'secularisation' or 'scientisation' (cf. ibid, p. 27). The aim of this method of analysing global relations was to move away from the separation of different disciplines of social sciences towards a universal analysis, embedded in history. Therefore, it is important to clarify that world-systems theory 'is not a subcategory of sociology' (Wallerstein, 2013, p. 1). It needs to rather be seen 'as a new perspective on social reality.' (Wallerstein, 2007, p. 1). As the term 'world-system' suggests, it is a macro-sociological analysis, which focuses on a 'capitalist world economy' in the context of a 'total social system' (cf. Martínez Vela, 2001, p. 1). Wallerstein points out that world-systems theory, or world-systems analysis, 'rejects the utility and even the validity of sociology today as an intellectual category, while acknowledging its continued strength as an organizational reality, and as a cultural preference.' (Wallerstein, 2013, p. 1). The use of the term 'world-system analysis' instead of 'world-system theory' is insofar more appropriate, as it highlights the importance of its consideration as a knowledge movement. Hence, Wallerstein indicates the primary strength of this analysis:

> it has resisted the temptation to define itself too narrowly and dogmatically, while still not allowing itself to be defined so loosely that anything that seems to deal with questions beyond the space of single nations/societies/social formations is deemed within the family. (Wallerstein, 2013, p. 7)

To analyse the world-system, a comparison of stakeholders of this system is also implied. Here, theorists not only talk about separated nations, but also about multinational companies as collective agents (cf. Faist, et al., 2014, p. 157). This cross-national relation often shows the 'development and unequal opportunities across nations' (Martínez Vela, 2001, p. 1). As a result, this 'combination makes the world-system project both a political and an intellectual endeavor.' (ibid).

Wallerstein classifies three key elements of world-systems analysis. First, the significance of the analysing unit. As mentioned before, the level of analysis of this Bachelor Thesis is not particularly 'a State/society/social formation' (Wallerstein, 2014, p. 4), but rather is based upon the context of a cross-linked system. For Wallerstein, 'world' cannot be understood as synonymous for 'global or planetary but simply to refer to a relatively large unit (relatively large in terms of area and population) within which there is an axial division of labor.' (ibid). Second, the world-system analysis is not everlasting. Besides world-system analysis, Wallerstein defines any system as following:

> They have lives. They come into existence; they pursue their historical trajectories within the framework of the rules that define and govern the system; and they eventually move so far from equilibrium that the system enters into terminal structural crisis. (Wallerstein, 2013, p. 4)

The third and final element is the rejection of the 'ontological separation of the imagined arenas so dear to the old dominant set of premises' (Wallerstein, 2013, p. 5). This means the denial of separated socio-cultural, political, and economical components. The main subject of the world-system analysis is the modern world-system, which originated in the sixteenth century. Its occurrence was geographically limited and could be traced back to European and American areas. Meanwhile, the world-system expanded over the whole globe and can be called world economy (cf. Wallerstein, 2007, p. 23/ Lee, 2011, p. 27). In this century, capitalism emerged and replaced feudalism (cf. Lee, 20011, p. 27). Like many other theorists, Wallerstein directly refers to a '*capitalist* world-economy' (Wallerstein, 2007, p. 23; italics in the original). Primarily, the world economy is a wide geographical area in which 'a division of labor and hence significant internal exchange of basic or essential goods as well as flows of capital and labor' (Wallerstein, 2007, p. 23) is focused on. Therefore, it could be suggested that the whole essence of the modern world-system is 'the axial division of labor' (Lee, 2011, p. 32). Because of the cross- or international character of a world economy, there is no binding to one specific political framework. It is a construct of many units in cultural, religious, and, therefore also, political ways. These units are 'loosely tied together in our modern world-system in an inter-state system.' (ibid). Wallerstein points out that a system can only be called a capitalist system if it has precedence on an ongoing growth of capital. This suggests that a capitalist system is only a phenomenon of the modern system. (cf. Wallerstein, 2007, p. 24). Hence, only a world economy can provide a framework in which a capitalist-system can exist. The main subjects of a capitalist world-system are markets and actors that compete with each other. At this point, we must focus on nations, as the most important actors of the 'capitalist-market game'. The playgrounds of this game are the economic and political fields. These fields are strongly connected to each other; they have a reciprocal relationship. In order to elaborate on this paper's analysis, the different spheres, Wallerstein differentiates in world-systems analysis are important to consider in order to understand cross-/international dynamics. He categorises core states, peripheral states and semi-peripheral states (cf. ibid, p. 29). Core states are the centre of economic power, and have control over the whole system; they are the economic leaders. On the contrary, peripheral states are on the fringe of the world economy. Peripheral areas are completely dependent on core areas and are controlled by them. The area in between is called semi-peripheral. Semi-peripheral states are pressurised by the other two spheres, because they need to focus on not shifting into the periphery, but moving towards the core. Consequently, they have the hardest challenge to deal with (cf. Wallerstein, 2007, p. 29). It is necessary to mention that boundaries between these spheres cannot be seen as equal to state borders, but rather as a 'mechanism per se that fragments the system into partially independent, semi-autonomous parts' (Lee, 2011, p. 33). Nevertheless, Wallerstein still sees the 'national states, or more precisely, the bounded territories over which national states attempt to exercise sovereignty' (Wallerstein, cited by Brenner, 2011, p. 116) as the elemental units. As can be reasoned from the above, a result of this system is a hierarchical order of various centres of power (cf. Brenner, 2011, p. 116). In the epistemological context, we can talk about state-centrism and its three essential assumptions. The first assumption refers to 'the conception of space as a static platform of social action that is not itself constituted or modified socially' (ibid, p. 108); 'spatial fetishism' is a result of this. The second assumption is 'that social relations are organized within territorially self-enclosed spatial containers' (ibid); this is what Brenner calls 'methodological territorialism'. The third and final assumption of the epistemology of state-centrism is 'that social relations are organized at a national scale or are undergoing a process of nationalization' (ibid); Brenner calls the result 'methodological nationalism'. The aim of this concept is the generation of an 'internalist model of societal development in which national territoriality is presumed to operate as a static, fixed, and timeless container of historicity.' (ibid). It is generally accepted that the concept of state-centrism is mostly relevant in political sciences, rather than in other disciplines of social sciences.

> States have been viewed as politically sovereign and economically self-propelled entities, with national state territoriality understood as the basic reference point in terms of which all subnational and supranational political-economic and sociocultural processes are to be classified. On this basis, the (national) state has been viewed as the container of (national) society. (ibid, p. 109)

Even if the unit of analysis goes beyond geographical borders, the approaches to world-society/system analysis will always be embedded in the epistemology of state-centrism (cf. ibid, p. 115). Therefore, the understanding of the space is 'on both global and national scales— as a timeless, territorial container of social relations.' (ibid). World-systems analysis can be interpreted as a response to critiques of dependency theory (cf. Thompson, 2015). However, Wallerstein's world-systems approach can also be criticised in this way. First of all, capitalism is not the only reason for underdevelopment and inequality. Any kind of conflict - ethnic, cultural, for example - can be causes for it. Furthermore, corruption plays a big role (cf. ibid); 'the game is never fair'. Wallerstein's focus on capitalism as the most dominant element is not always justifiable (cf. ibid). Another main element that Thompson brings up are religious regimes and their possible tyrannical characters. In addition, world-system does not include all areas. According to Thompson, the concept of the three spheres (core, semi-periphery, periphery) should be questioned itself. He criticises the stability of the approach, because it seems hard to test the theory in practice (cf. Thompson, 2015).

Related to the context of migration, world-systems analysis focuses on the question of 'how migration affects the character of relationships among countries, and among regions and cities within countries' (Bean & Brown, 2015, p. 72). Through migration, a particular relation takes place within the world-system; the one between receiving and sending nations (cf. Bartram, et al., 2014, p. 4). Wallerstein mentions that

> In general, the influx of workers from one country to another is a market plus for entrepreneurs in the receiving country and a market minus for those already resident in the receiving country, if one uses a simple short-run supply and demand model. This leaves out of the picture two elements that may very much be central to the debate: the impact on the internal social structure of any given country of immigration; and the long-run economic impact of immigration (which might be quite positive even if the short-run impact is quite negative, at least for some persons). Once again, there exists no neutral position. (Wallerstein, 2007, pp. 46-47)

At this point, it is unavoidable to categorise migrants as 'international goods' on the cross-national market. Hence, the ongoing analysis will concentrate on human-capital theory. While world-systems analysis already frames the theoretical basis of this Bachelor Thesis, human-capital theory will particularly put migration into focus. Accordingly, it is important to state that this Bachelor Thesis focuses on migration as a phenomenon in the world-system economy.

2.3.2. Human Capital Theory

Migration is a tool of the world-systems economy, and can be defined as human-capital. However, before there can be a closer look at migration as a form of capital, it is necessary to understand human-capital theory itself. The term 'human capital' directly refers to the labour market. Therefore, 'Human capital is the stock of skills that the labor force possesses.' (Goldin, 2014, abstract). Human capital can also be interpreted as an investment made by individuals in themselves to improve their own economic productivity (cf. Olaniyan & Okemakinde, 2008, p. 479). According to the Oxford Dictionary, human capital can be understood as: the skills, knowledge and experience of a person or group of people, seen as something valuable that an organization or country can make use of (Oxford Dictionary, human capital). The theory is 'based on the demand for certain skills and labour needs.' (Bartram, et al., 2014, p. 129) and has been developed by demographers and economists with the aim 'to examine the costs and benefits of immigration for destination countries' (Bartram, et al., 2014, p. 129). The concept of human capital was outlined or the first time in Adam Smiths (1776) *The Wealth of Nations*. Later, the economic embedding of the term was first made by Irving Fisher's *The Role of Capital in Economic Theory* in 1897. Using this work as a basis, in 1958 Jacob Mincer published his article *Investment in Human Capital and Personal Income Distribution*. After, Gary Becker's *Human Capital: A Theoretical and Empirical Analysis, with Special Reference to Education* in 1964 was essential for human capital theory. Theodore Schultz's 1961 published article *Investment in the Human Capital* was commented on by Golding as follows:

> Schultz's article (1961) demonstrates the importance of the concept of human capital in explaining various economic anomalies. Some are easy to figure out, such as why both migrants and students are disproportionately young persons. Some are more difficult, such as why the ratio of capital to income has decreased over time, what explains the growth "residual," and why Europe recovered so rapidly after World War II. Some are even more difficult, such as why labor earnings have risen over time and why they did not for much of human history. As is clear from most of these issues, the study of human capital is inherently historical. (Goldin, 2014, p. 2)

The assumption of this theory is that someone - a nation, a company, an organisation - can invest in people. This investment can, for example, be made in the form of training and education. The most important factor of this process is the aim of the investments; there needs to be a high probability of a constant positive result, or at least a continuing development. The aim of this investment is to increase the productivity of individuals (cf. Golding, 2014, p. 1/ Fix, 2018, p. 15). For many economists, human capital/ human resources are the factors on which a nation's economic and social character depends, not, as someone might expect, capital or material resources (cf. Olaniyan & Okemakinde, 2008, S. 480). The comprehension of personal income distribution is the primary approach of the human capital theory. Hence, individual income is seen as proportional to human capital (cf. Fix, 2018, abstract). Human capital theory and Marxist theory are quite similar. In Marxist theory, any value is produced by labour. Therefore, the productivity of 'high-paid skilled workers' must be higher than the one of 'low-paid unskilled workers' (cf. ibid, 2018, p. 17). Labour migrants are mainly motivated *'by the prospect of employment in another country.'* (Bartram, et al., 2014, p. 91; italics in the original). In general, labour migrants migrate from poor to wealthier countries (cf. Bartram, et al., 2014, p. 91). The migrant labour market in wealthy countries mostly contains requirements of physical labour. Therefore, human capital investment for men is higher than for women (cf. ibid, p. 92). As a result, in recent years destination countries have tried to manage labour migration as a way of controlling the flow by reducing lower-skilled or not required migrants (cf. ibid). Similarly, to other migration issues, it is clear that consequences of labour migration are primarily analysed in the context of destination countries. The effects for sending countries subject the dominant analysis of wealthy receiving countries (cf. ibid, p. 93). Amongst others, human capital theory has consensus with liberal progression and democratically ideologies, present in many Western societies (cf. Olaniyan & Okemakinde, 2008, S. 480).

Nowadays, education is the most effective form of investment. To determine the level of productivity of individuals, they can be classified and compared in various ways. This, for example, can be measured by people's level of income (cf. Goldin, 2014, p. 3). On the national market, the flow of human capital depends on institutional influence. Part of these enabling institutions are legal and extra-legal rules; the ability to determine property rights of people (cf. ibid, p. 5). Moreover, 'a host of related institutions such as the franchise, form of government (due process, rule of law), and religion.' (ibid) play an important role. Every investment wants to achieve an optimal result, and this depends on different factors. Economics, politics, and security - but also the efficiency of the market - contribute to these factors. An unequal balance of these factors leads to suboptimal accumulation of human capital. In the political context, for example, a reliable long-running commitment to the 'higher classes' cannot be made (cf. ibid). In relation to the context of migration, the investment in human capital achieves perhaps its largest form. Therefore, human capital theory attempts to explain the selective character of migration (cf. Castles, et al., 2014, p. 30). The extent of the investment in migration can be compared to the one in education: 'People decide to invest in migration, in the same way as they might invest in education, and they are expected to migrate if the additional lifetime benefits' (ibid). According to Castles, the expectation that people would migrate if migration was to bring benefits for the individuals is of an 'unrealistic nature' (cf. ibid, p. 31). Castles does not see migration as a result of rational actions. Potential migrants often do not 'have perfect knowledge of wage levels and employment opportunities in destination regions.' (ibid). Furthermore, the access to markets and their conditions are not perfect, so not everyone could easily access it. Castle criticises that 'neoclassical theories are often incapable of explaining real-life migration patterns' (Castles, et al., 2014, p. 31). This critique is not uncommon in human capital theory. Fix mentions that the human capital theory 'prevents the scientific understanding of income distribution.' (Fix, 2018, p. 15). One of his arguments regards the instability of the theory. The results can barely be underpinned by evidence, or they depend on 'circular reasoning' (cf. ibid). Another critique of human capital theory is its understanding of productivity as individual characteristic. Instead, productivity can be understood as a social characteristic (cf. ibid, p. 20). Therefore, it is important to consider the social background. Fix explains:

> Just as with hens, highly productive humans may actually be suppressing the productivity of others. This behavior would invalidate the premise of human capital theory (and much of neoclassical economics). (ibid, p. 21)

Another problem of the human capital theory is the growing divergence of the knowledge base and of the increasing learning effort of individuals (cf. Olaniyan & Okemakinde, 2008, p. 481).

2.4. Communities and Social Action

Durkheim notes that acts of observance complete the ideal power of symbol systems (cf. Durkheim, 2016). Since the emergence of societies, people have periodically come together to celebrate rituals and ceremonies. These collective actions 'fulfil the need to worship the sacred.' (Smith & Riley, 2009, p. 10). Consequently, 'a strong sense of group belonging' (ibid) was established. People use chants, incantations, and music to create an atmosphere of collective emotion (cf. Durkheim, 2016). This is what Durkheim calls religion. It 'is not merely a system of practices, but also a system of ideas whose object is to explain the world' (Durkheim 1968, quoted by Smith & Riley, 2009, p. 10). Every individual action can also be seen in a collective context, because of its impacts on the surrounding society. On the basis of this concept, Weber defines four types of social action. The first of these actions is labelled instrumentally-rational (*zweckrational*), defined as being

> determined by expectations as to the behavior of objects in the environment and of other human beings; these expectations are used as "conditions" or "means" for attainment of the actor's own rationally pursued and calculated ends (Weber, 1987, p. 24)

The second category is called value-rational (*wertrational*) actions. All actions which are *wertrational* are 'determined by a conscious belief in the value for its own sake of some ethnical, aesthetic, religious, or behavior, independently of its prospects of success;' (Weber, 1987, pp. 24-25). The third form are affectual or emotional actions. They are 'determined by actor's specific affects and feeling states' (ibid, p. 25). The last category are traditional actions which are 'determined by ingrained habituation.' (ibid). The first two categories dominate the social action analysis. While value-rational actions are driven by cultural goals and aims, instrumentally-rational actions are driven by the norms of capability (cf. Smith & Riley, 2009, p. 13). According to Weber, in modern society, social actions became more goal orientated (*zweckrational*) (cf. Weber, 1987). Weber and Durkheim agree with each other that religion is a central dimension of society and culture. However, while Weber focuses 'on the intellectual content of abstract belief systems' (Smith & Riley, 2009, p. 14), Durkheim centres his analysis on embodied emotions. In analysing religious dynamics and circumstances, Durkheim refers to sacred goals and moral ties (cf. Durkheim, 2016). In modernity, Weber points to 'disenchantment', a global loss of meaning (cf. Weber, 1987). As a consequence of Weber's understanding of the modern world, the religious meaning of actions and social relations has lost its 'positive' collective sense. This leads to many conflicts between individuals and within societies.

> A social relationship will be referred to as "conflict" (*Kampf*) insofar as action is orientated intentionally to carrying out the actor's own will against the resistance of the other party or parties. The term "peaceful" conflict will be applied to cases in which actual physical violence is not employed. A peaceful conflict is "competition" insofar as it consists in a formally peaceful attempt to attain control over opportunities and advantages which are also desired by others. [...] without a meaningful mutual orientation in terms of conflict, will be called "selection". (ibid, p. 38; italics in the original)

It is necessary to mention that, at the present time, not every case of social selection is a conflict (cf. ibid, p. 39). First of all, selection, or in this context social selection, means that some types of behaviour and personal qualities facilitate success more often than others (cf. ibid). In his analysis of social relations, Weber differentiates between communal and associative relationships. The first form is also called *Vergemeinschaftung*. These types of relationships can rest on many forms of traditional or affectual emotional bases. National community, loyalty, religious brotherhood and erotic relationships are just a few examples of communal relationships (cf. ibid, p. 41). On the contrary, associative relationships are based on a rational assimilation of interests and complementary motivated arrangements (cf. Weber, 1987, p. 41). These forms of social relationships are also called *Vergesellschaftung*. Weber differentiates three varieties of associative relationship. According to Weber,

> [t]he purest cases of associative relationships are: (a) rational free market exchange, which constitutes a compromise of opposed but complementary interests; (b) the pure voluntary association based on self-interest (*Zweckverein*), a case of agreement as to a long-run course of action oriented purely to the promotion of specific ulterior interest, economic or other, of its members; (c) the voluntary association of individuals motivated by an adherence to a set of common absolute values (*Gesinnungsverein*), for example, the rational sect, insofar as it does not cultivate emotional and affective interests, but seeks only to serve a "cause". (ibid; italics in the original)

In migration studies, social relations are the epicentre (cf. Brettell & Hollifield, 2015, p. 6). Only through an analysis of these relations can the migration process be understood. In the context of social, cultural and national identity, social solidarity is a major topic. '[T]he basis for social solidarity and cooperation is sometimes less secure than some would like' (Bartram, et al., 2014, p. 1). The insecurity of solidarity results from migration inflows, as well as from prejudices and preferences of native inhabitants.

3. The Ideological Character of Nationalism

This chapter explores the relation between ideology and nationalism. As one assumption of this Bachelor Thesis, the analysis of nationalism is embedded in an ideological context. Therefore, different understandings and interpretations of the term 'ideology' are outlined; historical aspects are also considered. Before analysing nationalism as a particular system of society, the terms 'nation' and 'state' are explained. In analysis, understanding of these terms usually differentiated. This thesis will explore why this is an important part of analysis. Subsequently, citizenship as a phenomenon, which emerged within the dynamic of state and nation, is referred to. The various analyses of nationalism, and therefore its theoretical approaches, are outlined. The relation between nationalism and the concept of identity are part of nationalism analysis. For this reason, it is examined in this Bachelor Thesis. Furthermore, diaspora theory, as a particular from of nationalism analysis, is considered.

<u>3.1. Theory of Ideology</u>

According to Wallerstein, an ideology 'is a coherent strategy in the social arena from which one can draw quite specific political conclusions.' (Wallerstein, 2007, p. 60). Ideological concepts go beyond a collection of theories and ideas. In addition, the analytical interpretation of ideology is not only applicable to a certain worldview or moral mission (cf. ibid). Wallerstein argues that, in previous and modern world-systems, there has been no need for an ideological understanding, until

> the concept of the normality of change, and that of the citizen who was ultimately responsible for such change, were adopted as basic structural principles of political institutions. (ibid)

Moreover, an understanding of ideology as a social function is quite common. In this context, the analysis of ideology takes into account how social functions are achieved (cf. Morris, 2009, p. 8). In Marxism, ideology is understood as being initiated by class interests. These interests are socio-economic, and cause conflicts (cf. ibid, p. 10). Morris draws similarities between Marxist understanding of ideology and the Freudian psychoanalysis of the defence and structure of the psyche (cf. ibid). The congruence can be determined in Freud's analysis of conflicting interpersonal factors. Therefore, Morris draws parallels between this approach and that which 'Marx explained for society as a whole.' (ibid). In addition to Freudian approaches, the concept of ideological rationalisation can be tracked back to psychic defence and socialisation. Following this assumption, the concept of superego influences the rationalisation process (cf. ibid, p. 11).

> Upholding ideological rationalization is fallacious reasoning commonly observed with ideological disputation and propaganda. A psychological understanding of ideology suggests that it is not an irrevocable alienating feature of social life and so may be escaped. (ibid)

According to Marxism, the capitalistic economic system creates its own ideology, allowing it to morally and psychically sustain itself. Therefore, ideology as a product of the capitalistic world economy plays an interactive role within the system (cf. ibid). In his analysis, Engels refers to the approach that capitalism as an ideology is a false consciousness. The ideology of capitalism can be defined as a mindset that contains the concealed interests of specific elite classes of society. As a result, individuals can be alienated from their natural requirements and can be misdirected in praxis. An example of this is the alienation of factory workers in the early industrial revolution. The workers 'were alienated by the environmental conditions of factory employment impairing their health and preventing them from enjoying the realization of human potentiality' (Morris, 2009, p. 40). As a response to the social condition of these workers, the, for Marxists, utopian ideology emerged (cf. ibid). In addition, capitalism's own ideology depends upon self-objectification (cf. ibid, p. 11). Morris claims that the Marxist tradition questions whether ideology can be strictly defined by wrong consciousness. This question is influenced by postmodern expressions. If this assumption is true, every 'ideology, including Marxism and variations of it, would be based upon a false consciousness of self, its social relation-ships and economic organization.' (ibid, p. 12). In sum, the core of Marx's analysis of ideology is psychological understanding and the identification of reasons for the misin-terpretation of social reality (cf. Morris, 2009, p. 17). The Marxist analysis of 'ideology as epistemological obfuscation class interests' (ibid, p. 40) is rooted in Western philoso-phy developed by Nietzsche. Nietzsche's theory can be referred to as an iconoclastic ap-proach. An analysis of class society is important for the conceptual understanding of Marxist ideology. Class society is strongly connected with class interests, as well as the division of labour. Within the context of economic human production processes, a con-sciousness of social reality is shaped. Therefore, one subject of analysis is people's ma-terial needs (cf. ibid, p. 41). Morris claims that

> [t]he universalization of an ideological belief convinces all competing social clas-ses that the interest of a dominant social class is the general interest of the whole society. Asserted as absolute truth, ideological beliefs lead believers to fatalistic ac-ceptance and social control by them. Ideologues, namely philosophers, priests, edu-cators and pleaders of special causes propagandize the ideological beliefs of the dominant social class (ibid)

The problem with the embedding of ideology in class society is the unquestioned division of control. As a result, dominating classes are able to control the entire system, while lower or victimised classes are manipulated by the ideological system. Here, the illusion of false ideological beliefs as a form of knowledge misleads believers. Consequently, they accept class interests, which are actually contrary to their individual ones (cf. ibid, p. 42). In modern sociology and political sciences, theorists tend to refute Marxist understanding of ideology and agree with Mannheim's conception of *Weltanschauung*. Without ques-tioning either this or the 'total conception' of Mannheim, 'the logical incompatibility of both conceptions' (ibid, p. 10) is not considered. The 'total conception' of ideology 'is relativistic, grounded in the presuppositions of scientific positivism, linguistics, structur-alism, historicism and postmodernism.' (Morris, 2009, p. 11). The analysis of Mannheim 'accepts the Marxian definition of ideology as a false consciousness of social reality that abortively attempts to reconcile opposed social interests that can only be resolved by revolutionary praxis.' (Morris, 2009, p. 13)

Mannheim's analysis of ideology is based on Hegel's dialectical theory. He focuses on epochal consciousness as a dialectical construct. Moreover, the relationship between the individual and their inhabited culture and society is an ongoing dialectic process (cf. ibid, p. 16). In relation to this, Mannheim has a specific understanding of a 'conflicting class-interest psychological perspective' (ibid). The 'total conception' and *Weltanschauung* of Mannheim interprets social reality, without considering truth claims (cf. ibid, p. 17). Morris states that Mannheim's particular conception 'treats knowledge, defined as enunciating truth, as a Marxist misconception.' (ibid). First of all, an ideology tries to protect and maintain social cohesion, to ensure the survival of the societal collective. The general assumption of this hypothesis is embedded in Mannheimian concepts, as well in Marxist-Freudian conceptions of false consciousness as ideology (cf. ibid, p. 116). According to this,

> Mannheim's Weltanschauung perspective describes ideology as a value-neutral given phenomenon without critically examining the social conditions of its origination. However, such a positivist phenomenological perspective ignores the causes, aims, values and consequences of ideology. Contrary to this, a Marxist-Freudian perspective questions ideology to reveal motives that conceal causes and promote deceptive perceptions of social reality. (ibid)

In general, two approaches of the studies of ideology exist. The first is the interest theory and the second, the strain theory. The background to interest theory is universal conflicts of advantages. In interest theory, the base is the constant attempt to remediate the sociopsychological imbalance (cf. Geertz, 1973, p. 201). The first theory focuses on the power conflict between individuals, while the second theory claims that they flee because of fear. Interest theory has two major problems. Geertz claims that 'its psychology is too anemic and its sociology too muscular' (ibid, p. 202).

> The clear and distinct idea from which strain theory departs is the chronic malintegration of society. No social arrangement is or can be completely successful in coping with the functional problems it inevitably faces. All are riddled with insoluble antinomies: between liberty and political order, stability and change, efficiency and humanity, precision and flexibility, and so forth. (ibid, p. 203)

According to Geertz, the aim of ideologies is the explanation of social situations. Furthermore, an ideology attempts to interpret social situations by the means of subconsciously goal-orientated actions within it. (cf. ibid, p. 220). According to Geertz, ideologies can be 'projections of unacknowledged fears, disguises for ulterior motives, phatic expressions of group solidarity' (ibid), but they are primarily 'maps of problematic social reality and matrices for the creation of collective conscience.' (Geertz, 1973, p. 202). In an attempt to explain the difference between ideology and sciences as cultural systems, Geertz points to the approach of symbolic strategies. From his point of view,

> Science names the structure of situations in such a way that the attitude contained toward them is one of disinterestedness. Its style is restrained, spare, resolutely analytic: by shunning the semantic devices that most effectively formulate moral sentiment, it seeks to maximize intellectual clarity. But ideology names the structure of situations in such a way that the attitude contained toward them is one of commitment. (ibid, pp. 230-231)

Geertz claims that scientific approaches are diagnostical and critical analyses are dimensions of culture. On the contrary, ideological approaches are exculpatory and defensive (cf. ibid, p. 231). Scientific analysis points to 'social element[s] in the pursuit and perception of truth, [and] its inevitable confinement to one or another existential perspective' (ibid, p. 197). Conversely, the analysis of ideology focuses on reasons for intellectual mistakes (cf. ibid). Ideologists do not prioritise the discovery of the truth or logical argumentation, but rather their own interests (cf. Morris, 2009, p. 105). Ideology cannot be interpreted as a form of science, since its background 'is linguistically based emotional persuasion disguised as truth-seeking debate'. (ibid). Some theorists argue that 'Ideology appears as knowledge if for no other reason that it is a set of beliefs often fiercely contested by argument and public debate.' (ibid, p. 17). Rationalisation is insofar implied in ideology, as ideological idea ignores, manipulates and falsify facts to promote ideological interests. In political debate, rationalisation plays a big role

> if it benefits a particular ideological position and it works [...]. The fallacy lies in approving of something for one reason, while disapproving of it for another. If the means secures one's interest, the means is approved, although illegitimate. Then there is the relativized truth rationalization (ibid, p. 106).

Historically, there are many examples that show, how ideology was used in politics to enforce self-interests. Therefore, propaganda became a tool to achieve self-interested goals (cf. ibid, p. 109). Some examples are 'Italian Fascism, German National Socialism, Russian Bolshevism, French and Italian Communism, the Action Française, the British Union of Fascists' (Geertz, 1973, p. 197). Political debate on ideology is often limited to a conceptual understanding of ideology. The debate often contains a categorisation 'of the vast array of political beliefs and historical social movements' (Morris, 2009, p. 12), which sometimes ignores a deeper understanding.

> Ideology could be defined as a set of socially shared beliefs culturally transmitted by natural processes of socialization. As such, ideology is an interpretation of oneself and one's social environment in the comprehensive sense of Weltanschauung. It orders the lives of individuals with a set of beliefs offering a lifestyle choice that also controls social behavior. (Morris, 2009, p. 13)

Therefore, the danger of ideology is the adaptation of a false reality. In this sense, ideology attempts to become an ultimate social knowledge in social reality. If this happens, the ideology would not need to approve itself anymore (cf. Dormal, 2017, p. 128). Another danger of ideology is 'depoliticisation'. In this case, circumstances seem to be unchangeable; no one needs to exert oneself for it. As a result, representation becomes a self-referential business (cf. ibid, p. 127). Morris suggests that

> [t]he concept of ideology is more significant and less prone to misinterpretation when it can be sharply distinguished from all political philosophies as well as religion, mythology and science. As a generic concept for disparate political philosophies, ideology disregards their truth claims, thereby making them seem relative and equivalent. A more significant conception of ideology would limit it to those propagandized ideas falsifying social reality, concealing motives and deceptively manipulating the gullible. (Morris, 2009, p. 10)

On the one hand, it can be argued that Morris' conceptual approach is important for rational analysis of ideology. On the other hand, it seems impossible to detach ideology from other cultural and social analyses.

3.2. State and Nation

The conceptual understanding of 'nation' and 'state' are closely connected with each other, but mostly are not composed of the same subject matter. The following subchapter analysis the relation of these terms. As outlined in the following section, historical impact and development of the nation and state concept are fundamental. For this reason, the role of 'legal membership' is explored and analysed, particularly citizenship in the form of double citizenship, as this highlights the inter- and transnational perspective of the previous chapter *2.2. Internationalism and Transnationalism.*

3.2.1. Idea of State and Nation

The search for a common understanding of 'nation', 'state' and 'nation-state' is the main problem of the nationalism debate. Many theorists agree that nation and state should be differentiated from each other. Otherwise, a congruent analysis would not be possible. In analysing the concept of state, the most dominant approach is an interpretation of 'a legal and political organization, with the power to require obedience and loyalty from its citizens' (Castles, et al., 2014, p. 64). In some analytical approaches, the focus on state-building is seen 'as a complementary project, aiming at the establishment of a political community of citizens, a forging of social solidarity, and respect and loyalty to state in-stitutions.' (Harris, 2009, p. 40). On the contrary, nations are seen as 'a community of people, whose members are bound together by a sense of solidarity, a common culture, a national consciousness' (Castles, et al., 2014, p. 64).

> The nation is a community of commonality, but so are many other communities. The specificity of this larger social grouping is in the emotional investment that it can extract from its members and in the solidarity that it can inspire. (Harris, 2009, p. 6)

While nations can be understood as a community with a shared common history and cul-ture, the state can be interpreted as legal concept. Harris identifies a particular territory and indicates 'the aggregation of political and administrative institutions' (ibid, p. 39). In modern society, nation-state is often used in analyses to highlight the conceptual fusion of nation and state. '[M]odern nation-state implies a close link between cultural belonging and political identity' (ibid). In this regard, Weber points to language as an important factor. From his point of view, based on a common language, the concept of state and nation-state have become analytically identical (cf. Weber, 1987, p. 395). Moreover, the role of power is important to analyse. Weber claims that the conceptual understanding of nation 'directs us to political power. […] The more power is empathized, the closer ap-pears to be the link between nation and state.' (ibid, pp. 397-398). The understanding of nation is, for many people, not firstly connected to 'people of a state'. In other words, nation is not equal to 'the membership of a given polity.' (ibid, p. 922). Even though, the concept of nation is strongly related to language, Weber argues that

> a "nation" is not identical with a community speaking the same language; that this by means always suffices is indicated by the Serbs and Croats, the North Americans, the Irish, and the English. On the contrary, a common language does not seem to be absolutely necessary to a "nation". (ibid)

In his analysis, he draws parallels between the idea of nation, and, therefore its advocates and 'prestige' interests (cf. Weber, 1987, p. 925). States depend on shared collective identity and their attribution of meaning. Therefore, the concept of state can also be understood as a product of nation-building and the emerging shared culture and politics (cf. Faist, et al., 2014, p. 134). 'Nation building stands for a deliberate effort to construct an overarching collective identity which can bind the political community in a more meaningful way.' (Harris, 2009, p. 39). Furthermore, the relation of state and nation can be understood to be dynamic.

> There is thus a sort of dialectic of state and nation. It is not just that nations strive to become states; it is also that modern states in order to survive strive to create national allegiances to their own measure. (Taylor, 2000, p. 202)

Wallerstein suggests that, while nations can be identified as a social construct of belief, states are the institutions that keep this construct alive.

> Nations are to be sure myths in the sense that they are all social creations, and the states have a central role in their construction. The process of creating a nation involves establishing (to a large degree inventing) a history, a long chronology, and a presumed set of defining characteristics (even if large segments of the group included do not in fact share those characteristics (Wallerstein, 2007, p. 54)

In the middle of the 18th century, the term 'nation' referred to a sum of people, living on the same territory. Smith claims that modern societies are the origin of many nations and also nationalism. According to him, the American and French revolutions were the starting point (cf. Smith, 2005, p. 24). In the 19th century, the term began to identify them not only externally, but also normatively and politically (cf. Dormal, 2017, p. 19). Dormal claims that the concept of nation belongs to the kind of inexplicable social phenomena that require more than a superficial definition (cf. ibid, p. 20). Dormal classifies the main question of the sociological understanding of nation as how the attribution of a specific feeling of solidarity is established, and how it works. Furthermore, sociology faces the question of why these attributions are successful, if they do not contain evident features, and how different forms of solidarity differentiate from each other (cf. ibid, p. 21). For many years, nation was an unquestioned established structure of organising a society. During the 20th century,

> new researchers appeared on the scene, and the informational base expanded. The need to explain and clarify the process of the formation of modern nations took on the aspect of a currently relevant task for the social sciences, and the study of 'nationalism' was raised to a political and ethical duty. (Hroch, 2000, p. 93)

For the first time, in the 1980s, the analysis of nation started to consider nation as a non-natural unit. The new debate explored the following core questions: Is the nation a product of modernity of is it deep rooted in history? Is nation real or fictional? (cf. Dormal, 2017, p. 22). The second question is related to the question of reality and fiction in the context of society itself. Dormal claims that it is important for subject analysis to put the debate of nation, and the term's definition, into the political context. From his point of view, the political perspective is the most essential. In this approach, he refutes the interpretation of nation as 'Staat-' or 'Willensnation'. Moreover, he faces the challenge of questioning which political problems of modernity the nation responds to, and how it is done or fails. According to Dormal, this is the only appropriate way to understand the nation, why it was established as a model of order, and how it has changed historically (cf. Dormal, 2017, p. 23). Hroch follows a similar historical approach. He classifies it as a

> certain theoretical conception: the view that the great social group known as the 'nation' was formed in historical time, that it really exists in the present and may thus serve as an object of empirical research far more conveniently than the irrational and foggy notion of 'nationalism'. (Hroch, 2000, p. 91)

According to Dormal, nation analysis contains four dominant political fields. The first one is the relation between nation and sovereignty. The second research field is the understanding of nationalism as a form of political mobilisation. The third field concerns itself with the way citizenship rights are institutionalised in the nation. Finally, the fourth field considers the function of the nation in the integration of class conflicts and the justification of social solidarity (cf. Dormal, 2017, p. 39). Dormal highlights that his analysis does not consider nation as a rational phenomenon. Some theorist claim that the concept of nation has a racist and folk ideology character, but Dormal refutes this approach. He argues that this approach contains the identification of physical features, rather than a political community. Dormal points to the pure societal and political character of nation (cf. ibid, p. 62). The existence of a nation is connected to its representation. Representation creates the relation between the nation as an imaginary origin and the empirical nation as a politically constituted reality (cf. ibid, p. 151). Dormal notes that the action and conflict features of representation construction arguments justify the basic existence of delimited political fields, but they cannot legitimise the strict form and division of them (cf. ibid, p. 247). As a result, there is no need for a concept of citizenship rights as an indivisible container, which someone accepts either completely or not at all (cf. ibid, p. 248).

One theorist who specifically uses the term 'nation-state' in his analysis is Meinecke. According to him, a nation that finds the medium of self-realisation in the state, and which is politically motivated by the idea of individual and collective self-determination, is called a nation-state (cf. Meinecke, quoted by Kunze, 2007, p. 28). Kunze states that, according to Meinecke, in the 19th century, the aim of national movement was to transform a culture-nation into a nation-state (cf. ibid). In this sense, many theorists agree that an establishment of a nation-state was, and probably will continue to be, rarely peaceful (cf. Wehler, 2016, p. 106). In the debate of nation-state, a consideration of transnational aspects is important. This perspective of analysis dynamics extends beyond the borders of a nation-state. Furthermore, it is an analytical perspective related to notions of political community and belonging that go beyond the concept of the nation as well as nationalism that transcends the territorial boundaries of states (cf. Faist, et al., 2014, p. 114). In the debate of migration, is that

> there are important international and sub-national influences on the politics of immigration and integration, that represent a challenge to the view centered on the nation-state. (Favell, 2001, p. 241).

One assumption of identifying the dilemma to be challenged by the nation-state, led to by migration,

> incorporation of the newcomers as citizens may undermine myths of cultural homogeneity; but failure to incorporate them may lead to divided societies, marked by severe inequality and conflict. (Castles, et al., 2014, p. 64)

It is hard to strictly define nation, state and nation-state entirely. Often, understandings and concepts are constricted and do not take each important feature into consideration. Therefore, putting this debate into the migration context leads to more confusion. It is only possible to make assumptions about self-constrained conclusive theories or analyses. Therefore, in this Bachelor Thesis, state is a concept of an entirely political arrangement, a current condition. On the contrary, nation will be understood as a framework, an ongoing process. Within this process, a sense of belonging and identity is constructed. Indeed, it is necessary to note that this is not a general understanding or definition of state and nation. It is only a base construct, to facilitate an analysis of the main subject of this Bachelor Thesis.

3.2.2. Citizenship

Citizenship can be defined as social status and as the general concept of the interpretation of social membership. With the naturalisation of immigrants, the meaning of citizenship has also changed (cf. Bartram, et al., 2014, p. 34). In general, people use citizenship status to identify national belonging. It is a legal status noted in the passport. 'In idealized understandings of the nation-state, individuals have a single, stable national membership that determines rights and constitutes identity' (ibid). According to Bosniak, citizenship has four particular components. First of all, it 'is a matter of formal legal status'; second, citizenship 'is a matter of rights'; third, it 'denotes active engagement or participation in democratic self-governance'; and fourth, 'citizenship has a subjective component that captures people's sense of identification and solidarity' (cf. Bosniak, 2008). Bosniak's definition of citizenship is 'tightly tied to a single national identity and nation-state.' (Bartram, et al., 2014, p. 36). Many theories on and interpretations of citizenship concern themselves with a singular national membership. The reason for this is the danger of 'transnational consciousness' and 'divided loyalties.' For the nation-state, it would mean an undermining of 'the nationalist ideal of cultural homogeneity.' (Castles, et al., 2014, p. 66). Castles categorises four ideal types of citizenship. The first one is the imperial model. In this model, belonging to a nation is equal to 'being a subject of the same power or ruler.' (ibid, p. 67). The imperial model has a particular ideological character. In addition, the existence of a powerful ethnic group or nationality preludes dominance over other groups. The imperial model can be associated with the former Soviet Union (cf. ibid). The second model focuses on folks or ethnicities. Therefore, national belonging is a matter of ethnicity. In this model, minorities are excluded from the nation and also citizenship. An example of this would be Germany before 2000, before it introduced its new citizenship rules (cf. ibid). The third model is the republican one. In this model, the nation is seen as a political community, whose basis is a constitution, citizenship and laws. The republican model follows political rules and includes the national culture. Historically, the American and French revolutions represent this model. Therefore, France is the most demonstrative example (cf. ibid). The last model is the multicultural concept. It attempts to 'maintain their distinctive cultures and form ethnic communities, providing they conform to national laws.' (ibid). The multicultural 'approach became dominant in the 1970s and 1980s in Sweden, the Netherlands, Australia and Canada' (ibid). The four ideal types of citizenship share that they are based on members 'who belong to just one nation-state.' (Castles, et al., 2014, p. 67). Contrary to these ideal types, there is a transnational approach to citizenship. In this model,

> identities of the members of transnational communities transcend national boundaries, leading to multiple and differentiated forms of belonging. Transnationalism could have important consequences for democratic institutions and political belonging in future. (ibid, p. 68)

In the context of migration, a debate about the loyalty of migrants exist. Hence, the question emerged as to whether people with double citizenship are committed to their receiving, as well as to their sending, country. Double citizenship is a tool for international analysis. On the one hand, it is possible to explore social and political practices of individuals, groups and organisations across borders. On the other hand, changes in political institutions can be analysed. Here, national belonging to emigration and immigration countries and, also in transit-countries, is subject to analysis (cf. Faist, et al., 2014, p. 113). Via double citizenship, states and institutions are made to deal with cross-border ties and the loyalties of citizenship. Double citizenship is accompanied by pluralisation of membership and belonging. This phenomenon expands over borders of nation-states (cf. ibid, p. 136). Some critics claim that the concept of citizenship itself excludes a double membership, and therefore refutes the idea of transnationality of citizenship. In contrast, some argue that in the context of a legal non-institutionalised citizenship the critic might be right, but there are also forms of citizenship which go beyond single nation-states. A pertinent example would be citizenship of the European Union (cf. ibid). Another point of view is to consider double citizenship not as being a transnational citizenship, but rather as being a trans-nationalised form of national citizenship. Therefore, the concept of double citizenship would not replace national citizenship. Moreover, it emerges as a co-existing modification of it (cf. ibid). For many theorists, an understanding of citizenship is an important cross-disciplinary research field. Some analysing units are:

> equal citizenship or democratic citizenship or social citizenship or multicultural citizenship, whether the preoccupation is with civil society citizenship or workplace citizenship or corporate citizenship or postnational citizenship (Bosniak, 2006, p. 11)

Citizenship includes some people, but excludes others. Therefore, as a particular understanding of citizenship exists in between a group, this understanding can become exclusive.

> Citizenship as an ideal is understood to embody a commitment against subordination, but citizenship can also represent an axis of subordination itself. The fact that

citizenship leads us in these contrasting directions is, in one respect, an idiosyncrasy
of rhetoric. [...] . To the extent that we express our ideals of justice and democratic
belonging by way of the concept of citizenship, we need to be particularly sensitive
to the questions of exclusion implicated in the discussion. Citizenship of, and for,
exactly whom? (Bosniak, 2006, p. 11)

Current literature on citizenship moves away from strict national interpretations of citizenship and starts to question it. An increasing number of theorists demand a new modern
definition of the term. As a result, terms like 'post-national citizenship', 'transnational
citizenship', 'global citizenship' have begun to be used in debates (cf. ibid, p. 30). Additionally, some debates about economic and social citizenship have emerged. These debates reflect the 'critique of the material exclusion of the disadvantaged' (ibid, p. 98),
whose aim is to eliminate exclusion via politics and the law.

> Some argue that the achievement of "equal citizenship" requires close attention to
> matters of economic justice; others maintain that the practice 'democratic citizen-
> ship' requires a citizenry that enjoys basic material security. (ibid)

The citizenship debate has split many theorists, depending on their research field. However, even theorists of the same discipline do not always share the same opinion or approach. Looking closer at Wallerstein's approach, it becomes clear that his analysis subject is the construct of sovereignty. From his point of view, sovereignty itself constructed
the concept of citizenship. He notes that it was an external and internal claim to authority
(cf. Wallerstein, 2007, p. 43).

> It was first of all a claim of fixed boundaries, within which a given state was sover-
> eign, and therefore within which no other state had the right to assert any kind of
> authority-executive, legislative, judicial, or military (ibid)

For Wallerstein, the main characteristic of sovereignty is that it is a claim in and of itself.
The problem with claims is that they are meaningless until others accept them. Moreover,
claims can be disrespected by others. However, this is less important than formal recognition of these claims (cf. ibid, p. 44). 'Sovereignty is more than anything else a matter
of legitimacy. And in the modern world-system, the legitimacy of sovereignty requires
reciprocal recognition' (ibid). Sovereignty can be understood as 'hypothetical trade'. In
this understanding of the term, two conflicting parties exchange recognition as a form of
strategy (cf. ibid). The concept of citizenship results from the idea of a sovereign people.
'To be a citizen *meant* to have the right to participate, on an equal level with all other
citizens, in the basic decisions of the state.' (ibid, p. 51; italics in the original). Faulks
points to the negative aspects of the established concept of citizenship:

Since the late 1980s, thinkers on the left have also embraced citizenship as a poten-
tially radical ideal. There have always been socialists who have seen the democratic
potential of citizenship. However, in the past, the general attitude of those on the left
was one of suspicion. Citizenship was seen as part of the problem rather than a so-
lution to the injustices of capitalism. Indeed, the rights of citizenship seemed to be
imbued with a capitalist logic. (Faulks, 2000, p. 2)

Faulks claims that citizenship always reflects a particular type and relation of governance. In his analysis, he questions 'what social and political arrangements form the context in which it is practised.' (ibid, p. 6). He criticises the lack of consideration of this issue in citizenship literature. In his analysis, Faulks suggests separation of nation and state from each other in order to achieve a better understanding of citizenship (ibid, p. 42). In this conceptual approach, the nation is defined as a synthesis of language and territory. There-fore, Faulks agrees with the definition of nation as cultural and pre-political status.

By pre-political I mean that the form and membership of the nation are determined
by geography and history, not by democratic deliberation. The state, on the other
hand, is essentially a legal concept. (ibid, p. 42)

As a consequence of not separating nation and state, nationality and citizenship are often confused with each other. Therefore, citizenship has achieved a political and cultural sta-tus (cf. ibid). The problem some theorists point to is that citizenship is not an inclusive concept 'which could bind people from different cultural backgrounds together,' (ibid). Unavoidably, citizenship, similarly to nationality, is racialised and made exclusive.

3.3. Nationalism

The debate of nationalism has become dominant in common world-systems ap-proaches. Related to the Olympic Movement, or moreover the Olympic Games, national-ism theory is subject matter of this Bachelor Thesis. Therefore, this chapter considers historical, as well as modern, approaches. Many classical theorists explored the phenom-enon of nationalism, and this is considered in the following chapter. The concept of iden-tity, as the essence of nationalism, is referred to. Parallels between citizenship, national belonging, and migration are drawn. In the subchapter *3.3.3. Diaspora and Diaspora Theory*, transnational communities are considered as an analysis subject. Again, a con-tention to previous subjects, such as citizenship and communities, is made.

3.3.1. Theory of Nationalism

In nationalism theories, theorists follow various approaches. One approach is to understand nationalism as a status-group identity (cf. Wallerstein, 2007, p. 54). According to Wallerstein, it could be argued that it is the most important factor in maintaining the modern world-system. Wallerstein claims that nationalism is based on sovereign states within an interstate framework. From his point of view,

> Nationalism serves as the minimal cement of state structures. If one looks closely, nationalism is not a phenomenon merely of weak states. It is in fact extremely strong in the wealthiest states, even if it is publicly invoked less frequently than in states of middling strength. (ibid)

An important concept within nationalist ideologies is the achievement of the congruence of nation, state, and different ethnic groups (cf. Azzellini, 2011, p. 5/ Wallerstein, 2007, p. 54). Therefore, they need to have the same boundaries. Hence, every 'ethnic group should constitute itself as a nation and should have its own state, with all the appropriate trappings: flag, army, Olympic team and postage stamps:' (Castles, et al., 2014, p. 65). In this context, nationalism is more of an ideological construct rather than a real condition. In a nationalistic sense, every 'ethnic group is a potential nation which does not (yet) control any territory, or have its own state' (ibid, p. 66). In this sense, nationalism can be understood as a concept of political legitimacy.

> Nationalism, so far the most potent principle of political legitimacy in the modern world, holds that the nation should be collectively and freely institutionally expressed, and ruled by its conationals. [...] Nationalism relegates religion to a secondary, and even inessential, principle of a stable and legitimate political order and thus challenges traditionalist conservatism (O'Leary, 2000, p. 40)

In reference to this, Harris analyses nationalism as a doctrine. His understanding is that nationalism 'can direct the vision for the future, it can be and is politics, and it can aid other ideologies or compete with them.' (Harris, 2009, p. 3). O'Leary points to pluralism as the 'major political benefit that nationalism has given to humanity' (O'Leary, 2000, p. 46). Orwell classifies nationalism in two specific ways. First of all, he understands nationalism as a common assumption of classifying people like insects. Moreover, he defines nationalism as a habit to identify oneself with a single nation or another unit (cf. Orwell, 2020, p. 7). In this sense, the individual puts themself into a context of achieving their own, but mostly the nation's, interests. Orwell identifies the problem and disregards the concepts of 'good' and 'bad', because everything is considered in each particular context of interests. In Orwell's analysis of nationalism, he points to the difference be-tween nationalism and patriotism. Some theorists assume nationalism and patriotism are similar and closely connected to each other. '[N]ationalism has become the most readily available motor of patriotism.' (Taylor, 2000, p. 202). Contrarily, Orwell conceptualises patriotism as a connection to a specific area and a particular way of living. Orwell argues that in patriotism, the accepted setting of the individual is considered to be the best one, but it is not necessary to force other people to accept the same setting (cf. Orwell, 2020, p. 8). According to Orwell, nationalism contains movements and tendencies. As examples of this idea, he comments on communism, political Catholicism, Zionism, anti-Semitism, Trotskyism and pacifism (cf. ibid). From his point of view, the concept of nationalism does not necessarily contain loyalty to a particular government or country, including the government or country of each individual. He claims that units of nationalism do not even need to be real. He mentions that Judaism, Islam, Christianity are all subject to passionate nationalist feelings, but their real existence can be justifiably questioned (cf. ibid, p. 9). In addition, Orwell considers the phenomenon of the immigrant status of many historical leaders of important nationalist movements. These people actually came from peripheral areas, in which nationality is an insecure element (cf. ibid, p. 17). To name just a few: Napoleon, Stalin and Hitler. One approach which would allow the classification of dif-ferent forms of nationalism is the concept of positive, transferred, and negative national-ism (cf. ibid, p. 26). As an example of positive nationalism, Orwell refers to neo-Toryism, Celtic nationalism, and Zionism. In this regard, the first example contains the intolerance towards a decrease in British power and influence (cf. ibid). The second form of positive nationalism is related to the belief in the past and future greatness of the Celtic people. This form has a strong racist undertone (cf. ibid, p. 27). Orwell categorises Zionism as the third form of positive nationalism, as it almost completely occurs within Jewish com-munities, and is therefore not a form of transferred nationalism (cf. ibid, p. 28). The most recognised transferred forms of Orwell's nationalism concept are Communism, political Catholicism, consciousness of skin colour, class consciousness, and pacifism. Some ex-amples of negative nationalism would be Anglophobia, anti-Semitism, and Trotskyism. Trotskyists are against Stalin, just like the Communists support him (cf. ibid, p. 34). Or-well claims that the similarity of these two political opposites is their obsessive fixation on a single topic: the same inability to form a truly rational opinion based on probabilities.

In contrast to Orwell, O'Leary claims that loyalty is one of the most important features of nationalism.

<blockquote>
Nationalism implies that loyalty to the nation should be the first virtue of a citizen. This idea has internal and external implications. It suggests that loyalty to the national community should transcend loyalty to more particular identifications, personal, cultural, economic, or political, and that members of one's nation have higher moral claims than members of other nations. (O'Leary, 2000, pp. 69-70)
</blockquote>

In his analysis of nationalism, O'Leary draws parallels with other '-isms'. Generally speaking, the ending '-ism' categorises a belief system, ideology, doctrine and/or particular intellectual current. O'Leary claims that nationalism, statism, personalism and cosmopolitanism 'have all attracted rational arguments and exponents' (ibid, p. 70). Therefore, nationalism cannot be solely criticised in its characteristics. O'Leary argues that thoughts can be related to the belief that nations can be loyal towards other nations. For this reason, he highlights the relation between nationalism and internationalism.

<blockquote>
[I]ndeed it is inter*nationalism* proper to observe (genuine) international law and to provide charitable assistance to other nations. In brief, liberal nationalism does not deserve the contempt with which Gellner wishes to be associated. (ibid; italics in the original)
</blockquote>

He claims that nationalism can also be considered within the global framework to create internationalism: a system of nationalisms that cooperate with one another. According to this, it can be argued that nationalism is always set in a transnational context. That 'behaviours of other populations strongly influence the ways in which a given population thinks and acts' (Beissinger, 2000, p. 185) is unit of analysis. Through a transnational understanding of nationalism,

<blockquote>
[a]nalogy and example are critical elements in the spread of nationalism, and nationalisms need to be understood as transnational and inter-related phenomena, not merely a collection of individual and isolated national stories. (ibid)
</blockquote>

In relation to this understanding of nationalism, Taylor assumes that religious fundamentalisms, nationalism, and proletarian internationalism should be considered to be a similar matrix. This may help 'to understand their interaction, that they are so often, in fact, fighting for the same space.' (Taylor, 2000, p. 214). In his conceptual approach of analysing nationalism, O'Leary focuses on the content of public policy and the concept of citizenship. From his point of view, both of these sectors are primary elements of nationalism. Furthermore, O'Leary agrees with Gellner's assumption, who criticises the tendency of a 'natural' interpretation. Both of them also criticise the adoption of false declarations, 'dark gods, and accidental-but-bad-ideas theories of the genesis and diffusion of nationalism' (O'leary, 2000, p. 77). O'Leary claims that nationalism and 'nations have not been permanent features of human history' (O'leary, 2000, p. 77). Contrary to Gellner, he underlines the dominant political character and therefore a conceptual understanding of nationalism as a political doctrine. Moreover, Beissinger points to the importance of politics in nationalism.

> Nationalism achieves political potency only in the form of collective discourse, mass mobilisation or state practice, although it manifests itself in other areas of social behaviour as well. (Beissinger, 2000, p. 171)

According to Beissinger, nationalism is a form of controversial politics (cf. ibid). He has embedded nationalism in a context of contestation and normalisation and refutes the assumption of nationalism as 'teleology of time zones and stages.' (ibid, p. 174). He claims that nationalism is a political activity, which contains two forms 'of interacting participants - those who defend a given order, and those who challenge it or are viewed as challenging it.' (ibid, p. 177).

> Unlike Gellner, I do not view nationalism merely as a principle or claim, nor do I view it as necessarily an industrial phenomenon per se. It is rather a set of political behaviours oriented towards certain objects in politics (ibid, p. 174)

Gellner's attempt to connect nationalism and industrialisation, on top of politics, is also criticised by Mouzelis. From his point of view, both phenomena are not always tightly linked. Mouzelis claims that industrialisation can be easily achieved without nationalism and vice versa (cf. Mouzelis, 2000, p. 158). According to this critique, Mouzelis underlines his own justification of Gellner's theory.

> First, he has stressed that he uses the term industrialisation in a broad sense [...] Secondly, he has pointed out that his theory focuses on the emergence rather than the subsequent diffusion of nationalism. (ibid)

In his analysis, Mouzelis agrees more with Weber's concept of nationalism. Mouzelis refutes the idea of a general and substantive theory of nationalism (cf. ibid, p. 163).

> In contrast to Gellner, I see his theory of nationalism not as a substantive theory but as an ideal-type - an ideal type which, in its conceptual ingenuity and heuristic utility, compares quite favourably with Weber's equally ideal typical theory about the connection between Protestantism and capitalism. (ibid, p. 164)

Some theorists identify an aim of nationalism in that nationalism is responsible for people of their collective fortune (cf. Harris, 2009, S. 4). In this regard, in a certain periods, nationalism is the answer to challenges of the collective. The political aspect of nationalism is again put into focus. It is related to every given political system, but mostly depends 'on the prevalent ideology of the time, which equally seeks to answer society's challenges.' (Harris, 2009, p. 8). Harris agrees with the assumption of sovereignty within nationalism. From his point of view, sovereignty is related to a particular area. Following this line of thought, 'nationalism is not limited to actions and policies of the nation in charge of the nation state' (ibid, p. 12). Harris claims that nationalism also contains actions and politics of other national groups, within the territory of the state. (cf. ibid). These national groups question the legitimacy or seek the same autonomy as the dominant nation. Therefore, nationalism can be understood as a political ideology or strategy, 'whose objective is the relationship between 'the people' and the state' (Harris, 2009, p. 24). On the contrary, nationalism theory also contains less approaches related to politics. These less political approaches interpret identity as 'something more than the mere membership in any existing state' (ibid, p. 25). They have their origin 'in the Enlightenment, but particularly in the rejection of its all-encompassing 'reason' as a mode of explaining all human affairs.' (ibid).

In the middle of the 19th century, nationalism research became a modern phenomenon for many theorists. After WW I, many nation-states were established, and nationalism research extended. The key matter in old nationalism research was the right of the people to self-determination. In the 1980s, nationalism research changed (cf. Wehler, 2016, p. 7). While old nationalism approaches tried to explore the role of nation as a subject, new nationalism research is focused on a mental framework. In old research, nations counted as natural certainties. In the same vein, an existing nation owns the right to its own state. Moreover, a nation creates idea and value systems which justify its existence, interpret its history, and framework its future (cf. ibid, p. 8). The basic assumption of old nationalism research is influenced by Marxist ideas. In this context, nation is understood as base and nationalism as superstructure. In modern nationalism research, the debate is epistemologically rooted in new constructivist ideas, which dissolve the supposed essentialism of historical phenomena (cf. ibid). In addition, the role of language became a particular part of modern nationalism research. Nevertheless, the old nationalism approach still dominates the debate, because of its historical importance. Wehler claims that nationalism concerns itself with the legitimised order of community and the legitimisation of its national order (cf. ibid, p. 11). Marx and Bourdieu argue that nationalism is a worldview and conceptual vision. Wehler points to many specific phenomena of nationalism: National Socialism, language development, Fascism, ethnic conflicts and protectionism, political religion, migration, minority issues, and war and genocide (cf.

Wehler, 2016, p. 12). Furthermore, various deflexions of nationalism exist. These include conservative, religious, fascist, liberal, cultural, political, communist, protectionist, separatist, regionalist, irredentist, and integrationist deflexions (cf. ibid). Wehler claims that nationalism means integrations and mobilisation of a major solidarity association, or nation (cf. ibid, p. 13). Therefore, the general aim is to achieve a legitimisation of political power. According to Wehler, nationalism emerged because of structural crises in early modern Western societies. In this sense, modern social scientists talk about a critical phase of 'fundamental uncertainty' of the 'rule of trust' (cf. ibid, p.17). The most dangerous problem of nationalism might be its tendency in crisis situations to turn into radical nationalism with an excessive program and politics (cf. ibid, p. 109).

In the nationalism debate, the question of globalisation always emerges. While nationalism mainly considers national areas, globalisation refers to international fields.

> Nationalism is an ideology that stresses the autonomy, independence and sovereignty of the nation. Globalisation on the other hand is a process that promotes international interconnectedness. (Halikiopoulou & Vasilopoulou, 2011, p. 1)

As two phenomena of the modern world, nationalism and globalisation are related to different common understandings. While nationalism analysis contains nation-state and national identity, the unit of globalisation analysis are global problems and flows (cf. ibid). In general, three dominant schools of thought in globalisation debate exist. First of all, 'hyperglobalists', who assume the eventual destruction of the nation-state. Then second, 'sceptics', who argue that the nation-state is not endangered, because nation-states are still powerful. Third, 'trans-formalists', who think that the answer of the globalisation debate 'lies somewhere in the middle, and that what is of most significance is the understanding of the ways in which these two concepts transform each other.' (ibid, p. 3). The relation between nationalism and globalisation is reciprocal. Nationalism and globalisation have shaped each other.

> Depending on 'what' one observes and 'when' one views these phenomena, they can also be understood as flexible, changing their character over time and across space in order to adapt to new circumstances. (ibid, p. 6)

In this context, the term 'pan-nationalism' emerged out of the dynamic of nationalism and globalisation. The aim of the pan-nationalism concept is the symbiosis of global and national dynamics (cf. Danielsson, 2011, p. 41). The origin of pan-nationalism is 'the search for identity, the fateful mixing of 'race-science' and geographical thought, imperialism and total war' (ibid, p. 42). Contrary to Arendt, Danielsson argues 'that the nation-state was less important to pan-nationalism, and, therefore, not something that needed to be sustained by pan-nationalists.' (Danielsson, 2011, p. 42). According to Danielsson,

> Pan-nationalism played a major role in both constructing and reifying 'biologised' identities. In an increasingly mobile world, the pan-ideologies emphasised the continuity of identity, despite major population movements and interactions. (ibid)

Pan-nationalism is often associated with political movements in Eastern Europe, Germany, and Russia that emerged in the end of the 19th century (cf. ibid, p. 43).

> One of the primary distinctions that filled the East-West containers was the contrast between (Western) political and (Eastern) cultural forms of nationalism. [...] Western political nationalism was progressive, modern, the creation of the present if not oriented to the future. The cultural form of nationalism, which according to Kohn emerged in the East, was a reaction to this, opposed to its core values and driven by a quite different dynamic. (Spencer & Wollman, 2005, p. 201)

In his analysis, Danielsson considers pan-movements in the context of transnational studies and diaspora studies.

> In pan-nationalisms – and I include here both 'diasporas' and 'transnationalisms' – the focus was the 'racialised' or 'biologised' nation. It is nationalisms, therefore, that seamlessly travel across borders – in the sense that 'biology' travels with the individual him or herself who migrates. (Danielsson, 2011, p. 56)

Globalisation and nationalism strongly depend on each other, because only through members of nation-states, the population 'effectively participate[s] in a global world' (Hutchinson, 2011, p. 97). In the modern world, in order to achieve their aims 'national elites must cooperate within an unstable environment that involves balancing global and regional networks.' (ibid).

3.3.2. Concept of Identity

The essence of nationalism is the national identity of individuals. On the one hand, nationalism can define people's sense of belonging, which helps them to feel included. On the other hand, nationalism has consequences for people who do not form a part of this belonging. Migrants especially face this problem (cf. Bartram, et al., 2014, p. 7). In a cosmopolitan understanding, 'national identity does not matter: we are all equal as individuals, as "global citizens" – and nationalism is something to be resisted or suppressed' (ibid). From this point of view, nationalism is reduced to its negative impacts, like war and genocide. As a consequence of international politics, 'deterritorialised nation-states' emerged (cf. Castles, et al., 2014, p. 41). After 1994, many leaders, like Nelson Mandela, achieved a non-racial national identity. The aim of this was the embedding of 'international human rights principles' to accomplish 'a basis for democratic legitimacy' (Klotz, 2013, S. 171). In old nationalism theory, the feeling of national belonging developed from a common origin, ancestry, language, religion and history (cf. Kunze, 2007, p. 28). A cultural national identity extends over state borders, and can endure long periods of political division and suppression. An example of the first case is the Italian and German case in the 19th century. The second case is represented by the Polish example between 1772 and 1918 (cf. ibid). Some theorists argue that the construction of a national identity is always connected to group or national identity. A creation of 'us' and 'them' leads to a specific, defined national identity. Therefore, the aim of nationalism is understood as

> constituting the nation itself, in other words, elaborating an "us" from a population separated by a multitude of divisions based on class, religion, local interests, etc. through the selection of a series of common elements of belonging (race or language, religion or history, etc.) and establishing, in parallel, a "them" as the archetype of the other or that which is foreign, as a negative mirror image of a common identity. (Máiz, 2011, p. 117)

In the modern world-system, a debate of double citizenship has emerged. According to Koslowski, 'this trend of states undermines the demographic boundary regime based on international norms that have developed over the past century.' (Koslowski, 2001, p. 220). In this approach, the ideal concept of national identity is vulnerable. As many theorists claim, nationalism and double citizenship, belonging, or identity are mutually exclusive. Furthermore, Gerrtz mentions that

> The first, formative stage of nationalism consisted essentially of confronting the dense assemblage of cultural, racial, local, and linguistic categories of self-identification and social loyalty that centuries of uninstructed history had produced with a simple, abstract, deliberately constructed, and almost painfully self-conscious concept of political ethnicity-a proper "nationality" in the modern manner. (Geertz, 1973, p. 239)

Hence, nationalism's concept of a strict defined national, or state, identity rejects a potential fluid transnational identity. In the context of migration, this conceptual understanding leads to various difficulties between theory and practice. Koslowski argues that

> [c]ontrary to the designs of sending and receiving states, the migrant's act of taking on two nationalities may be indicative of neither assimilation nor homeland political identification, but rather of multiple political identities, an ambivalent political identity, or even an apolitical identity. (Koslowski, 2001, p. 215)

While emigration hardly affects the identity of the involved country, those of immigration countries are strongly affected. Hence, debates of migration and identity mostly consider identities of migrants and immigration countries. Some theorists claim that in general, immigration countries tolerate migrants.

> Immigration may periodically have been welcomed, indeed organised, if it has been perceived to be in the national interest but care has always had to be exercised that immigrants were of the right type so that their entry would not subvert the existing, dominant and reified vision of national identity. In all of this the civic nation state has played a central role. (Spencer & Wollman, 2005, p. 214)

Identity is the essence of community. Hence, national identity can be understood as the entity of nations, or nationalism. Cultural features of ethnicity shape cultural identity, which is often understood as national identity. In this sense, 'components of ethnicity are myths of ethnic origin and election, and symbols of territory and community.' (Smith, 2005, p. 27). According to Smith,

> Symbols of territory and community take a variety of forms. They include emblems of difference (flags, totems, coins, ritual objects), hymns and anthems, special foods and costume, as well as representations of ethnic deities, monarchs and heroes (ibid, p. 28)

Communities like regions, states, religious orders, tribes, royal families, military associations, and sports clubs use these symbols to maintain a valid identity for members (cf. Herzmann, 2014, p. 97). Herzmann claims that the identification of individuals with the symbols of their community is not always strongly defined. However, he also argues that this can change rapidly if foreign symbols are forced on them, or if their symbols are not respected (cf. ibid, p. 98). Within a community, a particular network exists, which keeps the community alive. It is hard for an individual to be member of a community without participation in this network. Additionally, communities can be connected with each other. Mann categorises 'five socio-spatial networks of social interaction in the world today' (Mann, 2005, p. 281). First, the local networks, 'which for present purposes just means subnational networks of interaction' (ibid). Second, national networks, which contain structured nation-states. The third form of networks are inter-national networks.

> [T]hat is relations between nationally constituted networks. Most obviously, these include the 'hard geopolitics' of inter-state relations which centre on war, peace and alliances. But they also include 'soft geopolitics' between state (ibid)

The fourth are transnational networks, that go beyond national borders, being uninfluenced by them (cf. ibid). The fifth, and last category of networks, are global networks.

They 'cover the world as a whole - or, perhaps more realistically, they cover most of it.' (Mann, 2005, p. 282),

3.3.3. Diaspora and Diaspora Theory

The concept of diaspora has its origin in ancient Greece. The term 'diaspora' is derived from the Greek term 'diasperien', and can be translated as scattering, scatter, or split seed (cf. Harris, 2009, p. 145/ Castles, et al., 2014, p. 42). Earlier, the word was used in Hebrew scriptures to 'identified Jewish communities in Hellenic Alexandria. (Harris, 2009, p. 145). More specifically, diaspora was used to identify Jewish people after the destruction of the Second Temple of Jerusalem. In later periods, the concept of diaspora referred to religious minority communities. The recent conceptual understanding of diaspora is mainly used for ethnic, or ethno-religious, and national minorities in countries of their non-origin (cf. Faist, et al., 2014, p. 125). Diaspora refers to people who moved from their homeland. Often, diaspora communities were result of colonisation practices, because people were dispersed and displaced by force (cf. Castles, et al., 2014, p. 42). Members of diasporas are 'people of common origins who reside, more or less on a permanent basis, outside the borders of their ethnic or religious homeland' (Harris, 2009, p. 145). Moreover, diaspora can be defined as a collective of emigrants. From their own point of view, and the one of foreigner, diaspora members do not live in their imagined home- or native country. Furthermore, the emigrants are not assimilated in their receiving countries. A general feature of diaspora is their group-related political and religious goal-orientated character (cf. Faist, et al., 2014, pp. 125). In research, diaspora communities differentiate from other migrant communities, because of their particular features. For example, diasporas maintain transversal relations with members of the same origin ethnicity, who have settled in other countries. Therefore, a transnational sense of solidarity and empathy exists between different diasporas of the same origin (cf. Castles, et al., 2014, p. 42). In general, social sciences' analysis of diaspora communities focuses on heterogeneity. Therefore, ethnicity and nationality are essential analysis subjects (cf. Faist, et al., 2014, p. 125). According to political activists, other political movements or social practices are not a matter of the analysis. This, for example, excludes sexual orientation, gender status, and legal status (cf. ibid). According to Brubaker and many theorists, it is important to establish an understanding of diaspora in the sense of a political right or claim, rather than a tight concept of political and cultural communities. Furthermore, the term 'diaspora' is also used by nationalistic groups. These groups try to accelerate a building of a nation. However, the concept of diaspora is more extensive than some might guess. Some governments try to influence 'their' emigrants. They try to control their resources to establish a patron state. Through this connection, national governments want to achieve security for their ethnic minorities, who are settled in other countries. This cross-national phenomenon is also considered to be a diaspora (cf. Faist, et al., 2014, p. 126). Diasporas, as a concept of political mobilisation within transnational social areas, have consequences for the central political field of citizenship of their 'host-countries'. This includes equal political liberty, and, connected to this, democratisation, as well as rights, responsibilities and collective education (cf. ibid). In the 1980s and 1990s, diaspora studies focused on the role of emigrants and diasporas in the context of conflict emergence in their home country. Recent studies are more interested in the role of immigrants as mediators in physical conflicts. Other subjects of recent diaspora studies are the role of immigrants as development agent after the end of a conflict, as well as their role as agents of democratisation (cf. ibid). The main problem of diaspora studies is the impossibility of classification in the context of individual migrant communities. Therefore, rights of representation and rights of legitimacy cannot be quantified (cf. ibid, p. 129).

Diaspora communities, which represent themselves as ethno-national associations, are the most common type of collective transnational actors (Faist, et al., 2014, p. 134). In analysis, it is possible to categorise three forms of transnational groups which are a challenge for the emigration country. The first groups are organisations of refugees; the second, stateless diasporas; and the third, origin-related diasporas. Stateless diasporas often try to found a nation, or at least established a high level of autonomy, in their declared home country (cf. ibid, p. 135). These communities are mainly represented by organisations or, which could be considered, depending on the point of view, as liberation movements or, conversely, terrorist groups. Stateless diasporas are often connected to armed conflicts in their former home country, including certain Kurdish groups and Tamil organisations. In contrast, origin-related and established diasporas are often considered as strategic partners by their origin countries. The Armenian, Chinese, and Palestinian diasporas in the United States and Europe are some examples of origin-related and established diasporas. Established diasporas have particular characteristics. In the context of nation-building, they play an important role in national interests and national identity (cf. ibid).

We are in the realm of 'trans-nationalism' but, while the increased movement of ideas and goods across the globe – globalisation – may be responsible for the increased number of diasporas, the latter, unlike other movements, refers specifically to the combination of human experience and territorial dislocation, that is, the move from the 'home nation state' to the 'host nation state'. Diaspora is also an 'imagined community', but a word imagined is hardly ever more appropriate because 'imagining' in diasporic identity not only crosses the boundaries but creates a new identity, with a whole new dimension of being in diaspora. (Harris, 2009, p. 146)

In a contemporary understanding of diasporas, nationalism, and the transnational network, the role of ethnicity is questioned. Overlapping affiliations are produced by the cross-national link of people. The link goes beyond territorial boundaries of states and connects host societies with homelands (cf. ibid, p. 148). Consequently, Harrison puts forward following question: 'are we observing an emergence of a less national order or the return to atavistic primordial identities?' (ibid).

4. The modern Society of Sport

This chapter takes a closer look at sport in the world-system and the world economy. Hence, sporting capital is considered as special form of human capital. Moreover, the Olympics are explored. Current circumstances as well as ancient origins are explained. As an agent of the modern Olympic Movement, the IOC is analysed. Furthermore, religion is matter of analysis in this chapter. The reason for this is the tight connection of analysis of the Olympics and the religious character of nationalism.

4.1. Sport and Sporting Capital

In modern society, a career in sport is not uncommon. People are able to reach high and influential positions if they pursue a professional sport career. Throughout history, as society changed, sport changed as well. Traditional games transformed into modern sport, and a more transnational character was added (cf. Clastres & Bayle, 2018, p. 5). In general, sport has two dominant agents. The first one is the athletes, and the second is the clubs and organisations. 'Challenges between athletes and clubs were quite common as early as the 1860s, long before most national and international federations were formed.' (ibid). Sport became a world-wide trade. Therefore, the competitive aspect of sport led to an international trade of distinctions and awards between states and the sporting world (cf. Clastres & Bayle, 2018, p. 15). Eager for international recognition, a lot of 'sports executives are highly susceptible to honours, foreign decorations and honorary doctorates.' (ibid). Rowe claims that in modern society there is a market and exchange of sporting capital.

> Sport is a socio-cultural construct and any effective theory of sporting behaviour and its determinants must embed these aspects of the very nature of sport as an integral part of the theory. Sporting capital does this by addressing the particular and sport-specific factors that are influential in both the decision to participate in sport at any given time but also, importantly, the likelihood of sustaining that participation over time. (Rowe, 2017, p. 46)

In this theoretical approach, Rowe considers sporting capital as a form of human-capital, and draws parallels between these theories. He argues that human capital is an individual attribute, as is their sporting capability (cf. ibid, p. 47). Both forms are embedded in the economic context. For economists, education is an investment, which they make to professionalise the capital of individuals. This also includes sport education.

> Sporting capital incorporates elements of cultural, social and physical capital that operates in the social of sport with all its associated rules, regulations, conventions, social norms, gender and power relationships. (ibid, p. 48)

Rowe points to the dynamic between the different forms of sporting capital. He claims that economic capital can be transformed into cultural capital, which can easily be converted into social capital (cf. ibid, p. 49). He argues, for example, that a more qualified sporting capital can lead to a higher social status.

> This does not mean, however, that sporting capital is the same thing as cultural capital and that acquiring sporting capital necessarily or automatically increases cultural capital or vice versa. (ibid)

As a universal theory, sporting capital theory 'provides a holistic and integrated view of the determinants of participation' (ibid, p. 63). As aspects of this theory, 'the psychological, social and physiological characteristics of a persons' identity, lifestyle and relationship to others' (ibid) is considered. The aim of sport capital theory is capacity building. The theory

> shifts the focus of public policy from the short-term objective of increasing an individual's current participation in sport to one of building the capacity to participate in sport now and over the longer term. (ibid)

It is expected that a higher sporting capital leads to more frequent participation in sport. Furthermore, it is expected that this 'more frequent and sustained participation impacts positively to build and reinforce sporting capital in a virtuous feedback loop.' (Rowe, 2017, p. 63). Key elements of sporting capital theory are identity, self-esteem, and self-efficacy (cf. ibid, p. 74). This theory is trans-disciplinary. Therefore, research fields like 'psychology, sociology, behavioural and market economics, culture and anthropology and political science and biology.' (ibid) are combined with each other. Hence, the research perspective is socio-ecological, and extends 'from the intrapersonal to the interpersonal to the community and wider cultural context' (ibid).

In migration theory, the general centres of analysis are economic and political areas. However, in sport-migration theory, the structural conditions of elite sports are key elements (cf. Kukuk, 2015, p. 79). The structural conception of elite sports is different to the one of the labour market system. Elite sport is a social field that combines a set of values, norms, rules, and even a sports jurisdiction. Particular organisations such as specified schools, communities and associations are agents of the sports-migration field. Kukus claims that sports-migration, in particular elite sports, is actions orientated and contains voluntarily imposed constraints and restrictions (cf. ibid). The careers of elite athletes are limited to a certain part of life, mostly from adolescence to middle adulthood (cf. ibid, p. 89). In this time, athletes focus on the achievement of their ideal physical accomplishment. Therefore, their skills are compared in competitions through subsequent records and wins, which have a high symbolic value. The context in elite sports varies between the different levels. The most common level differentiations are systems of leagues, as well as, worldwide, continental, national, and regional competitions (cf. ibid, p. 80). Each time the skills of an athlete improve, he has the option to go on a higher level. With this change comes modification to rules, the attractiveness and desirability of clubs and trainees, and access to financial support (cf. ibid). The most professional levels of elite sport are international and global competitions. On this level, athletes, as representatives of their nations, compete against each other (cf. ibid, p. 81). The background of the international competition is composed of certain sporting, political and geographical restrictions that are related to the nationality of the individual athletes (cf. ibid). Kukuk argues that the 'code of win' cannot be limited to country borders, and elite sports enforce globalisation (cf. ibid, p. 99). He also points to the non-excluding character of elite sport. It is immune to non-systematic allocation criteria such as nationality, wealth, or age. But the non-exclusion only takes place, as long as the participants are able and willing to compete on sporting criteria (cf. Kukuk, 2015, p. 99). In this context, Kukuk criticises the anachronistic character of the Olympic Games. International competitions are organised by associations, and teams and individual athletes are assigned to only one nation. In the case of double citizenship, an athlete is not allowed to represent two nations (cf. ibid, p. 100).

> A competitor who is a national of two or more countries at the same time may represent either one of them, as he may elect. However, after having represented one country in the Olympic Games, in continental or regional games or in world or regional championships recognised by the relevant IF, he may not represent another country unless he meets the conditions set forth in paragraph 2 below that apply to persons who have changed their nationality or acquired a new nationality. (IOC, 2019)

Global sport, as well as the Olympic Games, is becoming increasingly multi-cultural and multi-local. Nevertheless, global sport is still dominated by Western hegemony (cf. Kukuk, 2015, p. 101). In this sense, elite sport is a tool of demarcation of nations. On the one hand, a clearly defined nationality is claimed, and a nation-state container thinking, which is represented by nation related flags, symbols and hymns, is constructed. On the other hand, the 'code of win' goes beyond territorial borders. No distinct division of political-administrative units exists (cf. ibid, p. 102).

4.2. The Modern Olympic Movement

The historical origins of the Olympics and the modern Olympic Movement are complex. Therefore, ancient Greek plays a role in the following analysis. The IOC is the main agent of the modern Olympics, and its establishment will be considered in this chapter. The modern Olympics will additionally be explained. The end of this chapter will clarify the importance of religion in the analysis of the modern Olympics.

4.2.1. Historical Impacts – The Ancient Olympics

Even though the Modern Olympics differ from the Ancient Olympics, they are still historically related to each other. Indeed, the Modern Olympics originate from Ancient Greece. Throughout history, sport has been connected to sacred occasions, religious rituals, and celebrations (cf. Reznik, 2017, S. 95/ Parry & Girginov, 2005, p 12). In ancient

Greece, the Olympic Games were established, to celebrated and honour the gods and goddesses of the time (cf. Miah & Garcia, 2012, S. 2).

> At the same time, sport was not only there to please gods, but also to please humans themselves; in this sense, it was a form of entertainment. In Antiquity, individuals were able to overcome their everyday life, their worries, and their utilitarian pursuits through sport. (Reznik, 2017, S. 95)

Although the Olympic Games became very well-know, they 'were neither unique in the Mediterranean area, nor were they the first athletic competitions.' (ibid, p. 96). They exist alongside three other 'Pan-Hellenic' Games (cf. Miah & Garcia, 2012, p. 2). Each of the four 'Pan-Hellenic' Games were established to honour a particular god. In the case of the Olympic Games the god being honoured was the head of Olympia – Zeus (cf. ibid). Although there is no singular agreed understanding of the first occurrence of the Olympic Games, it is understood that 'the first recorded Games were 776 BC' (ibid). 'The ancient Games took place in the heart of the Peloponnese, at the sanctuary of Olympia.' (ibid). Ancient societies were 'organized around religiously motivated stories, i.e. myths, [and] games were of course of heroic origin.' (Reznik, 2017, p. 97). Central to this time were 'narrations of the divine actions of gods in which mortal humans also took some part' (ibid). Reznik points to the stories of the Greek geographer Pausanias, who lived in the 2nd century AD. Reznik summarised Pausanias narrations as follows:

> According to a mythical story narrated by Pausanias, the first Olympic Games were organized before the Flood of Deucalion and the organizer was Heracles of Crete (not to be confused with the Heracles who was later to fulfill the 12 labors) [...] According to Pausanias, the organization of the games themselves happened after an argument between the gods Cronus and Zeus (Pausanias, quoted by ibid)

In Reznik's analysis, he claims that the original playfulness and piety of the Olympic Games was replaced by material interests (cf. ibid, p. 102). He argues that the economic character became dominant, triggered by the need for financial support to organise the Olympic Games (cf. Jakab, 2014, p. 249). The celebration of the games, and entertainment of the people, was deeply connected to an intense financial effort. Hence, athletes became ambitious, due to free meals and the potential to win bonusses. Moreover, the athletes' interest in economic and societal status grew, as they wished to achieve a better position in society (cf. ibid, p. 250). As a result, the original Olympic Games deteriorated (cf. Reznik, 2017, p. 102). According to Reznik, the original sense of the Games became lost. From his point of view, although they technically continued, 'they become a formality where the performances of athletes are reduced to mere numbers in statistics.' (ibid).

> When sacred things are turned into profane ones, noble ideas become shallow and
> ordinary. The Olympics cease to be sacred for people and are transformed into a
> formal matter. And thus, each athletic performance, no matter how superb, becomes
> only a statistical entry and after some time, it is necessarily overcome and forgotten.
> (Reznik, 2017, p. 102)

Nowadays, many theorists agree that the godly character of the Olympic Games has significantly decreased. However, some people still believe in the origins of the games. To this, Reznik argues that '[t]he aesthetic dimension of sport that was facilitated by religious ceremonies in the Ancient Greece is at present replaced by nature.' (ibid, p. 102). He claims that even the Modern Games can be understood as something that goes beyond entertainment.

> Although continuing to present the games as a hallowed means of promoting world
> peace, the Olympic movement has not explained how 'noble competition in sport'
> might achieve this pacifying end. By contrast, coherent ideas about the impact of
> sport on individual aggression and a nation's propensity to wage war have long had
> currency in the popular cultures of the western world. (Pritchard, 2012, p. 25)

In social sciences, the circumstances regarding democratic Athens are the central point of many analyses. The aim of these analyses is to explore the relation between sports and war. Here, the approaches differentiate from the ones of 'predominantly qualitative research of ancient historians' (ibid, p. 29). Pritchard claims that '[d]emocracy may not have changed the class background of athletes but it did transform war.' (ibid).

> 'The class background of Greek sportsmen has long been debated: one group of ancient historians has argued that upper-class citizens dominated or even monopolised
> athletic competition in archaic and classical Greece, while another has argued just as
> forcefully that the lower class competed as athletes in ever-increasing numbers'
> (ibid, p. 34)

Compared to the upper class, poor people did not have the same access to sport education. The reasons for this were mainly socio-economic inequalities (cf. ibid, p. 82). Poorer families had problems 'to pay the fees of teachers and needed to have their sons at home in order to keep farming or business interests going.' (ibid). Many upper-class families considered athletics to be a privilege of their own social class environment. Therefore, 'a person's pursuit of it was taken as evidence of his family's membership of the elite.' (ibid). Although, some lower-class families could have 'afforded to send their sons to these classes, they probably decided against it for fear of being inappropriately classified as belonging to the elite.' (ibid).

The ancient Games differ from the modern Games in various ways (cf. Miah & Garcia, 2012, p. 4). 'As the ancient Games grew, it added new disciplines, including chariot races, horse races and the pentathlon (discus, running, wrestling, javelin, jumping).' (ibid). These disciplines are the roots of modern Olympic sports. The first field, in which athletes competed, was athletics.

> The Ancient Greeks were serious about their athletics: this was no mere play. They were the first amongst humans to institutionalise play-like activities into 'athletics'—competitions as important to them as their art, their religion and their morality, in which a man could achieve distinction through his excellence against all others in equal competition. (Parry & Girginov, 2005, p. 24)

Furthermore, the ancient and modern Olympics are different in regard to the appearance of the athletes. While athletes competed naked in the ancient Games, in modern Games they wear clothes with national emblems, and sponsorship logos (cf. Miah & Garcia, 2012, p. 4). Different assumptions of why ancient athletes competed in the nude exist. One is that they tried to achieve 'a completely equal and non-enhanced playing field' (ibid).

> Others argue that competing in the nude was a way of acknowledging that the Games were first and foremost a celebration of the achievements of the human body, while others would note that this condition was required in order to ensure women, who were banned from the Games, did not disguise themselves as competitors. (ibid)

Another point of comparison between the ancient and modern Games are the rituals. Miah and Garcia argue that, in ancient Games, 'the rituals were structured around religious ceremonies' (ibid, p. 5). On the contrary, they suggest that in the modern Games, religion was replaced 'with nationhood and patriotic sentiment as the key unifying ritual.' (ibid). Both of them point to the parallels between the opening ceremony of the modern Olympic Games and military ceremonies. They claim that the national flags and hymns highlight a strong patriotic background (cf. ibid). According to Miah and Garcia, the most important difference between the ancient and modern Games is the international character of the modern ones (cf. ibid, p. 6). The modern Games

> emerge from an aspiration to improve the social and political conditions of the world, as opposed to the ancient Games' focus on Greek representation alone. Moreover, today's Games are accompanied by the Paralympic Games, which take place a fortnight after the Olympic Games. (ibid)

Reznik claims that the 'mythical depiction of the reality is a characteristic feature of Ancient Greece' (Reznik, 2017, S. 100). In this sense, Greek mythology explains the origin of the Games and their culture. Therefore, the traditional understanding of the games is embedded in a context of a tight and unquestioned bound between humanity and the sacred. 'Through the course of time, humans forget about their origins and become more focused on the every-day and profane matters.' (Reznik, 2017, S. 100). Reznik argues that humans need to be constantly reminded of their origins (cf. ibid). The origins of the ancient Games are also the origins of the modern Games.

4.2.2. The International Olympic Committee (IOC)

Most of the leaders in the sports industry started their career in the field of sports administration, but this does not mean that they have no sporting attributes. The second president and founder of the IOC, Pierre de Coubertin, 'was a true sporting "all-rounder", even if he never took part in any competitions' (Clastres & Bayle, 2018, p. 14). He played an important role in rebranding the Olympic Games and is called the father of the modern Olympic Movement (cf. Clastres, 2018, p. 33). He held 'the IOC presidency for 30 years, […] to forge and spread his conception of "Olympism".' (ibid).

> Olympism is a philosophy of life, exalting and combining in a balanced whole the qualities of body, will and mind. Blending sport with culture and education, Olympism seeks to create a way of life based on the joy of effort, the educational value of good example, social responsibility and respect for universal fundamental ethical principles. (IOC, 2019)

Coubertin's aim was to spread the Olympic message, and therefore the Games, all over the world. As a result, Coubertin criticised the growing economic and political characteristics of the Olympics. 'As early as 1908 Pierre de Coubertin expressed concern about the misuse of the Olympic project for political aims' (Parry & Girginov, 2005, S. 122). The Olympic Charter is the tool for spreading values of Olympism. The Charter prohibits 'any form of political dependence of members of the Olympic Family or the promotion of nationalism' (ibid). Because of this, it is an important framework for understanding Olympic Values. Some theorists argue that the Olympics and politics have always been closely connected to each other.

> Issues concerning states' presentation, flags, assertion of national identity, recognition and boycotts of political regimes, and promotion of social and economic values have accompanied the modern Games since their first edition in 1896. (ibid)

Representation of nationalism is both a signboard and a worry of the Olympics. However, to internationalise the Games, the different teams still belong to a specific nation.

> The Olympic project had been international since its launch in 1894, but, even though Coubertin had taken steps to develop the Olympics beyond Europe, this initial internationalism was limited in extent because the IOC remained, to all intents and purposes, European. Consequently, it was his successor's [Baillet-Latour] expansionist and colonialist approach that truly spread Olympism across the globe, and by the beginning of World War Two the IOC's membership had widened considerably to include officials from South America and Asia. (Carpentier, 2018, p. 108)

Furthermore, the IOC sponsored regional Games to promote participation in the Olympic Games. For this reason, Asian and South American countries became important actors in the internationalisation of the Olympics. 'Tokyo's election as the host city for the 1940 Olympics was an important step in this globalization process.' (ibid). While Coubertin always tended to hold the IOC meeting in 'Lausanne, Paris or the cities of France's allies, London, Rome or Brussels' (ibid, p. 116), Baillet-Latour wanted to hold them in various countries. He refuted

> to hold every second Olympic Session in Lausanne on the basis that it was more valuable for the meetings to move from country to country in order to promote the IOC with the local authorities (political, sporting and economic) and evaluate the development of sport in each country. (ibid)

For this reason, the IOC meetings between 1926 and 1939 were all held in Western Europe. Warsaw, Lisbon, Barcelona, and Oslo hosted IOC meetings (cf. ibid). In 1938, the IOC crossed the Mediterranean Sea for the first time, and held the meeting in Cairo (cf. ibid).

4.2.2.1. The Modern Olympics

The modern Olympics, and other institutionalised sports, are led by 'the presidents of the IOC and international sports federations (IFs).' (Clastres & Bayle, 2018, p. 2). They promote their sports, and organise international events. Furthermore, they introduce new organisational and economic models (cf. ibid). In modern sports analysis, there are some problems. One of the major ones, is also criticised by many theorists, is the separation of the history of sport and modern sport management. Theorists of each discipline rarely combine or consider both perspectives.

In earlier periods, a quarter of its members were aristocrats (ibid, p. 34). Nowadays, po-

tential IOC members are elected by present members. Hence, it is guaranteed that ac-

cepted members have the features the IOC considers as appropriate. (cf. ibid, p. 10). On

the one hand, this selection method has its advantages; for example, the uncomplicated

management of internal and external crises. On the other hand, because of this, the organ-

isation turned into an exclusive society 'that has struggled to accept greater democracy,

respond to a changing world, and wholeheartedly embrace the televisual and marketing

age.' (ibid, p. 11).

Until 1980, the rules, adopted in 1894, on amateurism were maintained by the IOC. In

the Olympic context, amateurism means that athletes are not allowed to receive money

for their capability. Amateurism provokes a controversial debate in both the Olympic and

sports in general. Some people argue that amateurism implies the participation of athletes

to compete in sports itself. According to former IOC president Avery Brundage, amateur-

ism is the essence of sport and the natural origin of the Games. He criticises the growing

character of professionalism and believes 'that there was no future for the Olympic Games

and television.' (Brundage, quoted by ibid, p. 11). In contrast to Brundage, other people

claim that amateurism excludes any athletes, who are unable to participate without finan-

cial support. They argue that amateurism 'exclude[s] lower-class athletes and ensure the

Games remained the preserve of "gentlemen sportsmen".' (Clastres & Bayle, 2018, p.

11). Consequently, the debate of amateurism and professionalism is a controversial de-

bate, and opinions strongly depend on the dominant perspective of an individual. Never-

theless, in the modern Games, professionalism is common. The reason for this growth is

the dominant influence of politics and economy, and their influence both outside and in-

side the Olympic society.

A number of elite athletes have also risen to the top of sports administration, often after following successful careers in politics or business. Avery Brundage, who presided the IOC from 1952 to 1972, competed in the 1912 Olympics, Lamine Diack, IAAF president from 1999 to 2015, was a champion long jumper, and Sebastian Coe, the IAAF's current president, won athletics gold at the 1980 and 1984 Olympics. In fact, the most powerful position in world sport, IOC president, is currently held by a former Olympian, Thomas Bach. (Clastres & Bayle, 2018, p. 18)

The five Olympic rings are one of the most famous Olympic logos. The IOC refers to the five rings as the official Olympic symbol. The term 'symbol' implies more than just a commercialised meaning. In the IOC's understanding, the rings embody Olympic ideals (cf. Miah & Garcia, 2012, p. 12). Every ceremonial instruction of the Games follows a strict protocol that is consistent from one Game to another. One example is the lightning of the torch. It 'always takes place within the ancient grounds of Olympia where the flame is kindled using a parabolic mirror and rays from the sun.' (ibid, p. 14). The critique of the Olympics is growing.

> For example, the motto "citius, altius, forties" (faster, higher, stronger) is often misinterpreted as an explicit reference to the excess that elite athletes pursue in their attempts to do better than their predecessors or their previous performance. (ibid, p. 21)

Many theorists argue that the origin of the motto is an educational institution. Historians in particular claim that the motto 'appeals to far broader principles of life than the pursuit of athletic endeavour.' (ibid).

Because of the internationalisation of the modern Olympic games, a 'desire to record results' (Miah & Garcia, 2012, p. 7). Not only athletes, but also nations, compete with each other in the modern Games. The aim is to establish 'a hierarchy and selection system for international competitions.' (ibid).

> As far as it can be ascertained, the first in-depth study of the economic and social impacts of an Olympic Games was conducted by Ritchie and Smith (1991) on the 1988 Calgary Winter Olympics. The issue of the environmental impact gained recognition in a similar vein and since the mid-1990s environmental protection has become the third dimension of the Olympic Movement alongside sport and culture. (Parry & Girginov, 2005, p. 92)

At the end of the 20th century, after the post-industrial revolution, cities were constrained 'to re-define their image by developing policies aiming to compensate for reduced public expenditures, and equally to bring in more inward and foreign investments.' (ibid, p. 93). Therefore, the Olympic Games were used as catalysts to promote economic growth. The Games have the 'potential to generate business activities, such as job creation or tourism, and to contribute to the feel-good factor.' (Parry & Girginov, 2005, p. 93). The aspect of the financial effort of the Games is an often an unnoticed factor. 'Sending more and better-prepared athletes to the Games is an objective of many NOCs but it comes at a price.' (ibid p. 98). Concurrently, the

> expenditure associated with the participation of a national team for the Games, such as pre-Games competitions and training camps, hospitality and communications, represents a significant part of the investment flow to the local economy. (ibid, p. 98)

Hence, it seems that the trans-national extent of the Olympic Games results in a drifting apart of the original thoughts of the Olympics and their modern understanding. On the one hand, the cooperation of nations seems to increase. On the other hand, nations seem to focus more and more on their own interests.

4.2.3. The Olympics and Religion

In sports analysis, many approaches, which explore the relation between religion and sport, exist. The former IOC president and founder of the modern Olympic Movement, Pierre de Coubertin, claims that the ideal understanding of sports is a belief system. Coubertin introduced Olympism as an ideology of modern sports, and society. From his point of view, the term 'relegio athletae' identifies the belief of elite athletes. The aims of the athletes are fairness, positive results and the achievement of participation at the ritual of the Olympic Games. Jirásek criticises the simplistic understanding of the term 'relegio athletae' and he argues that it is much more complex than previous linguistic concepts consider.

> This topic has been addressed by experts in kinanthropology (e.g., sport science, human movement science, and philosophy of sport) but less often by specialists in religious studies, theology, and similar disciplines. (Jirásek, 2015, p. 292)

Contrary to simplified understandings, Jirásek argues that the term is not religious, and that 'it does not deal with holy, deity, or sacral spheres' (ibid). As a result, the combination of religious and sporting disciplines is barely realistic. Geertz mentions that the conception 'that religion tunes human actions to an envisaged cosmic order and projects images of cosmic order onto the plane of human experience is hardly novel.' (Geertz, 1973, p. 90). From Jirásek's point of view, he understands Coubertin's traditional attempt. Coubertin's analysis is based on the connection of modern sport and the ancient Olympic

Games. Jirásek admits that in ancient times, this might have been a justified approach, because 'all pan-Hellenic games were organized as religious ceremonies, celebrations, and glorifications of gods' (Jirásek, 2015, p. 293). However, according to him, Coubertin's assumption fails in modernity, because of 'completely different social conditions and lifestyles as well as the secularization of society and education' (ibid). The transferral of ancient features can lead to misinterpretations of Coubertin's original message.

> Although the goal of Coubertin's effort was education through sport, we should say that he used the idea of a modern religio athletae as a metaphor for the non-religious spirituality of sport. (ibid)

Jirásek agrees that the term 'relegio athletae' can only be understood 'as a symbol, metaphor, model, and image of an idea' (ibid). Otherwise, according to him, the analysis of the modern Olympics fails. Hence, the ancient Olympic belief system, which was naturally religious, is not equal to the belief system of the modern Olympics, even if modern Olympic theories use religious terms. 'From the beginning, interpretation of Coubertin's religio athletae was done from an educational and moral viewpoint, not a religious one.' (ibid). Additionally, in the context of the ideology of Olympism, a religious context should be avoided (cf. ibid, p. 294). Many theorists 'agree that Coubertin's religio athletae as part of the ideology of Olympism should not be perceived in a religious context.' (ibid). Moreover, they understand Olympism to be a form of 'social philosophy that emphasises the role of sport in world development, international understanding, peaceful co-existence, and social and moral education.' (Parry & Girginov, 2005, p. 2). As a concept of Olympism, the Olympic Movement 'worked for a coherent universal representation of itself' (ibid). De Coubertin represented this opinion of a universal connection between cultures. Through this understanding, the philosophy of Olympism is valid 'regardless of nation, race, gender, social class, religion or ideology' (ibid). According to Parry and Girginov,

> The contemporary task for the Olympic Movement is to further this project: to try to see more clearly what its Games (and sport in wider society) might come to mean. This task will involve both ideas and action. If the practice of sport is to be pursued and developed according to Olympic values, the theory must strive for a conception of Olympism that will support that practice. The ideal should seek both to sustain sports practice against unjust criticism (where it exists) and to lead sport towards a vision of Olympism that will help to deal with the challenges that are bound to emerge. (ibid)

Even though some theories avoid the understanding of sport as a form of religion, some of them admit that sport can 'be interpreted as an attempt to develop a religious attitude that is based on mutual respect and overcomes confessional differences' (Jirásek, 2015, p. 294). Jirásek argues that these aspects do not feature common 'characteristics of a true religion' (ibid). Geertz understands religion as a symbol system, which creates an omnipresent, powerful, and enduring motivation and atmosphere (cf. Geertz, 1973, S. 90). In this sense, a conception of a common system of existence is formulated. Furthermore, according to Geertz, the conception is embodied by many factors in order to validate motivations and beliefs (cf. ibid). Due to Geertz's understanding, it is not surprising that many people embed the Olympics in an entirely religious context. Jirásek argues that Olympism might suggest a religious context, but it is moreover a framework. Jirásek interprets Coubertin's theory as follows:

> Coubertin did not want to establish a real religion as an autonomous belief that is expressed by the relationship to the transcendental but grounded in the revival of the purpose of human existence. (Jirásek, 2015, p. 294)

On the one hand, religious ceremonies and the traditions of the Olympic Games facilitate a religious understanding of them. On the other hand, they can become instrumentalised. Sport events have already been used for 'religious propaganda, as a means of mission or, more particularly, as evangelization' (ibid). Jirásek claims that the common celebration of religious ritual, such as 'athletes making the sign of the cross, holding their hands toward heaven, falling on their knees' (ibid), is the reason for the embedding of the Olympic Games in the religious sphere.

> Superficially, these acts may appear to be examples of how religious rituals permeate sporting events. Such quasi-religious phenomena lead to an understanding of the role of religion in sport. (ibid)

One possible reason for the understanding of sport as religion might be spirituality. The Olympic Values are not just a motto; for some people they are a way of life. They have a spiritual background and spirituality

> can be understood as a symbol of searching for the purpose of life, the awareness of the depths of life, the unravelling of the ethical and aesthetic dimensions of the world, the desire for harmony, and the experience of transcendence. (ibid, p. 295)

In the context of the Olympics, Jirásek calls it a non-religious spirituality (cf. ibid, p. 296). According to him, the difference between this and 'real' religious manifestations is the internal factor of the Olympic non-religious spirituality. Moreover, he identifies it as 'a phenomenon that directly and inherently co-creates the substance of human movement in all areas of human movement culture, including sport' (Jirásek, 2015, p. 296). While the 'idea of establishing Coubertin's religio athletae as a real religion has been considered absolutely unrealistic, the same thing cannot be said about the spiritual values.' (ibid). Jirásek claims that sport can make people's lives more meaningful and 'fill the human experience with spiritual values' (ibid). Similarly to Jirásek, Reid refers to the spirit of the Olympics. He identifies the Olympic Ethos as the basis of the modern Olympics.

> However, though any religious ritual, no matter how apparently automatic or conventional (if it is truly automatic or merely conventional it is not religious), involves this symbolic fusion of ethos and world view, it is mainly certain more elaborate and usually more public ones, ones in which a broad range of moods and motivations on the one hand and of metaphysical conceptions on the other are caught up, which shape the spiritual consciousness of a people. (Geertz, 1973, p. 113)

According to Reid, Olympism is an important feature of modern sports, 'especially its philosophy and enduring spirit adds value to sport as a human practice.' (cf. Reid, 2017, p. 172). Reid argues that the ethos of the Olympics 'is distinctively humanistic and virtue-seeking; as such it enhances the social and educational potential of sport.' (ibid, p. 172).

In order to explore if the Olympic Games and the Olympic Movement strengthen nationalism or promote internationalism, it is important to consider and compare different statistics and data. Financial effort and migrant athletes are the central focus of the analysis. In some statistics, the term 'immigrant' is used, instead of 'foreign-born'. The reason for this is that some researchers use 'immigrant' in their analysis to include migrants of later generations, whereas 'foreign-born' generally refers to athletes that were not born in their representative country. Even though this Bachelor Thesis focuses on the analysis of foreign-born athletes, the term 'immigrant' is used, if it is also used in the original statistic. This avoids data falsification. One thing that approaches of migration research in sport have in common is their emergence in modern society. To approve current statements of the immigrant athletes (IA) debate, researchers collect various scientific data. Because of particular approaches and 'aims' of the data gathering, it is necessary to compare the different sources. The analysis of the migrated athlete phenomenon might be a modern trend, but it is hardly an occurrence of modernity.

> It is often believed that the Olympic Games have become more migratory. The number of Olympic athletes representing countries in which they weren't born is thought to be on the rise. It should, however, be noted that migration in the context of sports is hardly a new phenomenon. (Jansen & Engbersen, 2017, abstract)

In 2017, Jansen and Engbersen published their paper *Have the Olympic Games become more migratory?*. This was a big achievement for the data collection of migrant athletes in sport. Their subject of analysis is the common assumption, that the Olympic Games have become more migratory. Contrary to this assumption, they claim that the Olympic Games have not necessarily become more migratory. According to Jansen and Engbersen, the migration phenomenon in modern Olympics needs to be differentiated from the past. In modern society '[m]igration in the context of the Olympics is above all a reflection of global migration patterns.' (ibid, p. 12). As one conclusion of their research, Jansen and Engelsen argue that

> in the history of the Olympic Games, the selected countries have always been represented by sizeable amounts of foreign-born athletes. Olympic migration during earlier editions can to a great extent be characterised as European and colonial. Nowadays, in the epoch of diversity, foreign-born athletes come from all corners of the world. (ibid)

According to a report published in 2008 by the New York Times, the U.S. 'is a magnet for attracting accomplished veteran athletes to switch citizenship' (Wilson & Lehren, 2008). This report declares that since 1992, about 10 athletes from China and 40 from other countries have become U.S. citizens in order to compete in the Olympic Games (cf. ibid). Many countries are criticised for filling their Olympic Teams with foreign-born athletes. This debate mainly focuses 'on non-Western athletes (e.g. Chinese table tennis players or long-distance runners from Kenya).' (Jansen, et al., 2018, p. 524). Fahey argues that

> naturalized citizens have long been a crucial addition to national teams, and the per-
> centage of Olympians born outside of the country they represent has been growing
> slowly in recent years for most major teams. (Fahey, 2016)

Many people question the position of different agents in the Olympic field towards migration. According to some critics, agents are 'increasingly inclined to adopt an instrumentalist stance towards migration and citizenship.' (Jansen et al., 2018, S. 524). For example, the phenomenon of instrumentalisation becomes visible when states take advantage of migration by 'offering citizenship to talented immigrants so as to increase their global economic competitiveness' (ibid). Therefore, many people claim international sport is a global business (cf. Knott, 2011).

> It features multi-million dollar investments, corporate brands and rivalries, global
> media coverage, and – because of its rewards, and potential for reputation and power
> – an undercurrent of corruption and cheating as well as first class entertainment and
> excellent individual and team performances. (ibid)

As a result of the globalisation of sport, international sport organisations were founded. The IOC and FIFA (Fédération Internationale de Football Association) are the most famous ones, but the International Cycling Union and the International Cricket are also global agents,

> which manage and regulate the industry, and oversee global competitions such as the
> World Cup, the Olympic Games, the Rugby World Cup, test matches and Twenty20
> tournaments, and the Tour de France. (ibid)

Knott indicates 'first, the *migration of players*, and, second, the *transnational movement of fans*' (ibid; italics in the original), as the biggest problems, which emerge because of the growing globalised character of sport. 'In many team sports there is now a global market for the buying and selling of players.' (ibid). According to Knott,

The Baseball Factory, produced by David Goldblatt for the BBC World Service in 2008, revealed that in America's national game, almost half of all professional baseball players came from overseas, with about 40 per cent coming from the small Caribbean state of the Dominican Republic. (Knott, 2011)

The foreign-born athletes often receive a high salary for changing the country they compete for.

5.1. Financial Effort of the Olympics

Since 1960, the cost overruns of the Olympics have changed (Table 9). With cost overruns of 720%, the Montreal Summer Games in 1976 had the highest unforeseen spending. The Barcelona Summer Games (1992), the Lillehammer Winter Games (1994), and the Sochi Winter Games (2014) had a similar cost overrun. With just 2%, the Beijing Summer Games (2008) had the lowest cost overrun. In addition, the Vancouver Winter Games in 2010 (13%) and the Salt Lake City Winter Games in 2002 (24%) have been two of the Olympic Games with the lowest cost overruns. In general, the Summer Olympics have had more unforeseen costs than the Winter Games. With a total overrun of 176%, the costs of the Summer Olympics have approximately 30% more unforeseen spending than the Winter Olympics (142%). It is striking that the cost overruns in past Summer Olympics were more irregular than the ones of the Winter Olympics. With an average of 176% and a median of 83, the uncalculated spending of the Summer Games varied greatly. On the contrary, the average overrun costs of the Winter Olympics with 142% lay closely to the median of 118. In the past, the revenues of the Olympic Games have also grown. During 1993 and 1996, the marketing revenues of the Olympic Games were approximately 3.000 $ (Figure 1). However, between 2009 and 2016, the marketing revenue sum increased to almost 8.000 $. Figure 4 shows the growing revenue of the Olympics. Due to television right fees, the revenues of the Olympic Games have recently enormously grown. From 1960 to 1980, the broadcast revenues were quite low. After 1980, revenue quickly grew due to television right fees. In 1960, only 0,1 million $ were generated, while in 2012 it was approximately 2.6 billion $. Overall, the broadcast revenues from television rights fees of the Summer Olympics are much higher than those of the Winter Olympics.

During the history of the Olympic Games, medal bonuses were established to attract athletes. Table 8 shows six examples of bonuses for athletes in the year 2018.

Singapore and Indonesia make the highest investments for medal winners. The prize for gold, silver, and bronze medals is a six-digit figure. Gold medal winners of the Olympic Team of Singapore even get 1 million $. Compared to this, the USA, Germany, and Canada award five-digit medal bonuses. With the 9th rank, USA comes before Germany (11th rank), and Canada (12th rank).

<u>5.2. Migration in the Olympic Games</u>

Jansen and Engbersen's analysis, published in 2017, considers 'approximately 40,000 participants from 11 countries who participated in the Summer Games between 1948 and 2012.' (Jansen & Engbersen, 2017, abstract). As a result of their research, they argue that

> the Olympic Games indeed have not become inherently more migratory. Rather, the direction of Olympic migration has changed and most teams have become more diverse. Olympic migration is thus primarily a reflection of global migration patterns instead of a discontinuity with the past. (ibid)

Jansen and Engbersen outline the percental participation of foreign-born athletes from 1948 to 2012 (Table 1). In 1948, irrespective of the data of UNK (University of Nebraska at Kearney), the Great British Olympic Team had the highest percental rate with 10.2 %. Next to Brazil, with no foreign-born athlete in their 1948 Olympic Team, Spain (1.5%), Sweden (1.7%), and Australia (2.7%) also had very low percental rates. In addition, Argentina, with 3.5% foreign-born athletes in the Olympic Team, was below the 5.5% mark. The percental participation of foreign-born athletes in the USA Olympic Team never overstepped 8.1% (2012), and never fell below 3.8% (1964). From 1948 (5.5%) to 1958 (4.3%), the participation of foreign-born athletes in the Canadian Olympic Team fell by 1.2%. In 1960, the participation of foreign-born athletes in the Canadian Team increased to 18.8%. Up until 2012, Canada was one of the Olympic Teams with the highest percental rate of foreign-born athletes. The lowest was 13.9% (1964) and the highest, at the Olympic Games after that, was 23.7% (1968). Jansen and Engbersen's research also analyses the diversity of foreign-born athletes in 1960 and 2012, of particular Olympic Teams (Table 2). The closer the outcome to 1, the higher the diversity of the foreign-born athletes of the team. In 1960, Canada and Great Britain had the same high diversity of foreign-born athletes (0.898), directly followed by Australia and the United States (0.860). On the contrary, Spain had no diversity, because only one foreign-born athlete competed for the Spanish Olympic Team. In 2012, Australia, Canada, France, Great Britain, Italy, Spain, and the United States had a higher outcome than 0.9 in terms of the diversity of foreign-born athletes in their Olympic Teams. Brazil was the only country in Jansen and Engbersen's research that had in 2012 (0.560) a lower diversity than in 1960 (0.667). In general, the diversity of foreign-born athletes of the countries evaluated by Jansen and Engbersen in Table 2 was higher in 2012 than in 1960.

Table 3 shows the movement of foreign-born Olympians in 1960 to Europe, North America, Oceania, and South America. Jansen and Engbersen focused their results on the Olympic Games in Rome, during the first epoch after WWII. Considered in this context, about 55% of the foreign-born Olympians in these Games originated from Europe. In the 1960 Rome Games, the major of foreign-born European Olympians, originated from African countries (37%), while 35.6% originated from other European countries. On the contrary, North America, Oceania, and South America had no athletes from African countries. In 1960, 0.8% of foreign-born athletes originated from Oceanian countries. All of them competed for North America countries. With a percental rate of 3.7%, of all foreign-born athletes of North American Olympic Teams, Oceania originated athletes had the same rate as foreign-born athletes from other North American countries. In the 1960 Rome Games, foreign-born Olympians competing for South America only originated from Europe and South America. In Table 4, the outcomes show the cross-national movement in 2012. Most foreign-born athletes still originated from European countries, but only 36.8% of the total. With over 20% each, the foreign-born athletes in 2012 originated from Africa and North America. Hence, while in 1960 more than 50% of foreign-born athletes originated from European countries, in the 2010 Games more athletes originated from African and North American countries. As already concluded from Table 2, the total rate of Table 3 shows the growing diversity of foreign-born athletes in the Olympic Games.

Overall, around 8100 IA out of 109,000 Olympians - whose place of birth is known (OPB) - have participated in the Olympic Games since 1896 (cf. Mallon, et al., 2017). This is a percentage of 7.4%, and approximately '1 of 13 Olympians can be considered an Immigrant Athlete.' (ibid). Table 5 shows the leading nations of the highest percental rate of IA from 1896 to 2017. With their Olympic Team being composed pf more than 40% IA of, Qatar holds the highest position. Even though the Canadian

Olympic Team has had the most IA (637) since 1896, its total current percentage of IA (16%) is lower. Cyprus has the least IA since 1896. However, with 14 IA of 96 OPB, its percental rate (14.6%) is higher than Greece (14.5%), New Zealand (13.6%), and Hong Kong (13.3%). In general, since 1896, the Czech Republic, Jamaica, and Kenya have sent the most Olympians to compete for other countries (Table 6). According to the percental rate, Georgia and Serbia send the most Olympians to compete for other countries. The total number of OPB competing for these countries is made up of 30% IA. The outcomes of the research approach in Table 7 show the most common combinations of origin and receiving countries since 1896. The data in this table does not consider political connections between nations. The first rank of common nation combinations are athletes that originate from Jamaica and go on to compete for Canada. Canada has another common source of foreign-born athletes: Norway. This combination is rank 10 in the list of the most common nation combinations. Moreover, many athletes born in Norway, compete for the United States (rank 2). The United States has three other common countries from which their athletes tend to originate: Japan (rank 4), Ireland (rank 5), and Mexico (rank 6). In general, the nationality switches of Olympic Athletes between 1948 and 2016 grew (Figure 6). Until the Games in 1984, there were no more than 5 nationality switches per Game. In 1952, there was no switch at all. At the Games in 1996, the number of nationality switches increased to 15. In 2000, almost 30 athletes switched their nationality, and in 2004, more than 30. Until today, this was the highest number of nationality switches since the Games in 1948. After this, the number of switches fell, but it has never been less than 10.

The majority of foreign-born athletes in the U.S. Team compete in synchronised swimming and table tennis (Figure 3). About 50% of athletes in both disciplines were born abroad. Cycling, rugby, and swimming have the lowest rate of foreign-born athletes (lower than 5%) of the competing team. However, there are also disciplines in which the U.S. Team has no foreign-born athletes competing. Some examples are boxing, field hockey, and golf. Aside from the many disciplines in which foreign-born athletes compete for the U.S. Team, they are also one of the countries that loses the most athletes (Table 10). Besides Canada and Russia, in the 2018 Winter Olympics in South Korea, they had the highest loss of native athletes. With 37 U.S.-born athletes who competed for other nations, the U.S. has the highest rank just above Canada (21) and Russia (19). The three top countries in the 2018 Games that used foreign-born athletes, were South Korea itself (18), Canada (13), and Germany (11). Furthermore, at the same Games, 12 countries entirely composed of IA competed (Table 11). Thailand and Nigeria started with a total number of four athletes each, all of them IA. Morocco and Bolivia had an Olympic Team of two IA. In addition, Malta and Eritrea, for example, started with just one athlete at the 2018 Games, both of whom were born abroad.

5.3. Changing Nationality

It is often questioned why athletes compete against the countries they were born in. The debate about the nationality of IA is one of the biggest in global sport. Some people suggest that the athletes compete for other countries 'either because of heritage or because it may be the only way they could compete in the games.' (Vasilogambros, 2016). One example of an athlete who competes because of his heritage is Giovanni Lanaro. He is an Olympic pole vaulter who 'was born, raised, educated, and trained in southern California' (ibid). Nevertheless, in the 2016 Rio Games, he competed for Mexico. 'While he is an American, his mother was born in Mexico, and the Mexican national team only requires that you have Mexican heritage in order to compete for them.' (ibid). For individaul athletes, there is always a reason for switching, be it financial, cultural, or even career orientated. Mostly, individual cases of nationality switches, or competing against the country of origin, receive positive feedback. However, negative critiques are increasing against nations that recruit athletes from other nations. Mass requirement of athletes is not a one-off case. 'Azerbaijan, for its part, has heavily recruited foreign-born athletes; half of its 50-person national team in the 2012 Olympics were naturalized citizens.' (ibid). Furthermore, the Olympic Team of Great Britain started with 60 foreign born athletes in 2012 (cf. ibid). In the debate about Britains behaviour, *The Telegraph* even called IA 'Plastic British' (cf. ibid). In the U.S., foregin-born Olympic talents are already classified as people with 'extraordinary' skills, which qualify them for EB-1 visas (cf. ibid). 'While competing for a different country can raise an athlete's international profile, it could lead to criticism, as well.' (ibid). In the context of the 2016 Olympic Games in Rio, the *The Atlantics* writer Matt Vasilogambros mentions that

> [i]n the first modern Olympic games in 1896 in Athens, athletes by and large were not grouped by nations. Hungarian athletes were the only ones who competed under a national banner. It was a competition among 280 athletes in 43 events. It was not a competition among nations, even if they came from 14 different nations. In this Olympic games, 11,000 athletes will compete in 306 events under the banner of 206 nations. In the eyes of the athletes competing under the flag of a

country that's not home, they're competing in the Olympic spirit as much as anyone else. (Vasilogambros, 2016)

In a *CNBC* article of, Chemi and Fahey criticise Middle Eastern nations for buying 'top-notch African talents' (cf. Chemi & Fahey, 2016). In their arcticle, they argue that the Olympic Track and Field Team from Bahrain 'is composed primarily of runners from Kenya and Ethiopia, along with more from Jamaica, Morocco and Nigeria.' (ibid). According to them, the team has almost no native runners. However, Bahrain is not the only nation to be heavily involved in the trade of foreign-born athletes. The 'nearby countries [of] Qatar, United Arab Emirates and Turkey have also all been known, in the past decade, to pay to import elite athletes.' (ibid). Consequently, the purchase of elite athletes leads to a controversial debate. To avoid criticism over nationality, Qatar carries out a name change of foreign-born athletes. 'In 2000, Qatar bought an entire weightlifting team from Bulgaria, which helped it win a bronze medal by Angel Popov, competing under the name Said Saif Asaad.' (ibid). The following describes the case of Saif Saaeed Shaheen, who was born Stephen Cherono in Kenya and is now an athlete of the Olympic Team of Qatar.

> He was not well-known in Kenya, where there is such a surfeit of world-class runners that few qualify for the national team. Hardly anyone took notice when Cherono switched his citizenship and name in exchange for a lifetime monthly salary of $1,000 and the standard complement of elite trainers and cutting-edge facilities. But then he started winning races. In a surprise victory at the World Championships in Athletics, held in Paris that spring, Shaheen broke the world record for the 3,000-meter steeplechase. After crossing the finish line he fell to his knees and began to cross himself, but an official rushed to stop him; he then took a Qatari flag, wrapped it around his shoulders, and ran a victory lap; when he stepped up to the podium he forgot his new name and had to check the scoreboard. His brother, a runner on the Kenyan team, finished fifth in the same race, and refused to congratulate him. (Provan, 2011)

For nations that expect athletes to change their name after the nationality switch, this means that the Olympic Team becomes more hegemonic in its representation of its sending nation at the Games. For many athletes, there is no other option than fulfilling these requirements, because in some 'countries like Kenya and Ethiopia, where there is so much talent depth, cracking the country's top three just to qualify for the Olympics is a difficult task.' (Chemi & Fahey, 2016). In 2018, Brandon Wiggins wrote in his article *Why some Olympians can compete for countries they are not from:*

> For many athletes, changing their national allegiances is the only way to keep their
> Olympic dreams alive, especially if their home country is stacked with talent in their
> particular sport. (Wiggins, 2018)

Even if athletes fulfil requirements, such as name changes, they do not have complete permission to participate in the Olympic Team. An example is the case of Mushir Salem Jawher. He was a runner

> for Bahrain in a marathon in Israel. He said some things to the press about Israel that
> didn't go over well with the big brass in Bahrain, and as a result got his citizenship
> revoked. He begged his home country Kenya to take him back, and eventually com-
> peted again, this time for Kenya, under his original name Leonard Mucheru. (ibid)

Citizenship fast-tracking of is one of the main criticism surrounding debates over nationality change. An article from *SBS News* published in 2015 claims that 'Foreign-born athletes will have their Australian citizenship fast-tracked so they can represent the nation at international sporting events under proposed new laws.' (Anon., 2015). Australia acts ambitiously in making nationality switches for foreign-born athletes and skilled labourers easier (cf. ibid).

5.4. Nationalism or Internationalism?

The controversial debate over nationalistic characteristics in the Olympics is legitimate. Because of its historical background, nationalism is often put in a negative context. A reason for this is that nationalism is mostly understood as something that separates nations from each other, and strengthens the structures within each individual nation. In an interview, Frank Bockrath stated that in the 19th century, the traditional understanding of nationalism in sport started to transform (cf. Bockrath & Forudastan, 2004). He argues that, on the one hand, modern sport is composed of nation-states. On the other hand, global structures are strengthening. According to Bockrath, national representing and internationalisation go hand in hand in the Olympic Movement, as well as other modern sport fields. In his interview, Bockrath refers to the Esperanto movement, the German Red Cross, and the Boy Scouts as other international movements which originated from the *ideologischen Weltanschauung* (ideological worldview) in the 19th century. The Olympic Games also originated from this ideological interpretation of life (cf. ibid). Bockrath claims that in this century, the thought of internationalism had already reached nations and simultaneously national awareness strengthened. It is a plausible assumption that a nation needs to define itself more specifically if it increasingly becomes a single agent of an extending global network. Bockrath labels it as tension ratio (cf. Bockrath & Forudastan, 2004). The tension ratio is reciprocal and is context in which the Olympic Idea is embedded. As can be concluded from previous chapters, capitalism, nationalism, commercialism, and professionalism are part of the modern Olympics. The Olympic Games is clearly a competition. Contrary to common understandings, the Olympic Charter determines that

> [t]he Olympic Games are competitions between athletes in individual or team events and not between countries. They bring together the athletes selected by their respective NOCs, whose entries have been accepted by the IOC. They compete under the technical direction of the IFs concerned (IOC, 2019)

According to this paragraph of the Olympic Charter, the performance of athletes is a higher priority than national representation. It could be suggested that the modern Olympics represent a misinterpretation of the actual meaning of the Games. The Olympic Charter especially notes that countries do not compete against each other, but national representation is nevertheless a dominant characteristic of the Games. As can be concluded from previous chapters, this has two main causes. The first reason is on the micro-level. It is the representation of the cultural heritage of the athletes. Because of the growing trade of athletes, those unwilling to switch their native Olympic Team - not even for a particular amount of money - might strengthen their national feeling. It cannot be denied that athletes also participate because of national awareness, and '[d]espite the Olympics' best efforts, national pride and patriotism are now engrained aspects of the Games.' (Davis, 2018), not only related to the athletes themselves, but also to the spectators of the Olympic Games. 'Citizens may interpret the Olympics as a forum of showcasing their nation's strength and skill rather than a platform for international competition.' (ibid). Moreover, the second cause is that nations force nationalism in order to strengthen their representation in global competitions.

> Historically, nations have always jumped on the opportunity to show their strength, whether that be in battle, technology, or wealth. Sports are no different, with citizens uniting behind their athletes in international competition to fulfill national victory. (ibid)

In a time of growing global competition, of which the world economy is a prime example, nations have to assert themselves. Based on the assumption that the Olympic Movement originated from purely ideological thoughts, and not economic or political reasons, the Olympic Games became just one of many playgrounds for this global competition.

Therefore, the Olympics are connected to politics and the economy. Some people claim that the modern Olympics developed entirely because of economic and political causes. Therefore, '[f]rom a realistic and commercial point of view, the nationalistic media focus makes a lot of sense.' (Davis, 2018). Inevitably, it cannot be denied that the modern Olympic Games are a tool of global politics and economy. Hosting and participating in the Olympics has a big influence on a nation's economy.

> The Olympics have become a national rather than individual event. Hosting the event is not an act of hospitality but national pride. It must be grand, expensive, crush the city's budget, and enrich a network. The desire to see people with great strength, when combined with a global technology, hides more than it reveals. (Friedman, 2016)

Some nations have excellent native athletes and some nations need to recruit athletes from other countries to increase their chances of global success. It would be untrue to assume that nations only take the needs and desires of their athletes into account. Athletes need to be successful to compete for a national Olympic Team, and each nation wants to increase their chances of being one of the best Olympic Teams. The trade of foreign-born athletes is one of the global phenomena of modernity.

> Since the start of the modern Olympics, the glory and the sorrow were not simply the property of the athletes, but of the nations that competed. It was cast not as a trial of men (and later women), but a competition between nations. Victory was measured by a collective count of the medals won. Nations with more medals saw themselves – and were seen – as possessing some virtue other nations lacked. The nationalisation of sports changed the games profoundly. In a strange way, victory validated a nation. This is seen from 1896 onward, but it was the 1936 Berlin Olympics that definitively transformed the games into a national and ideological contest. (ibid)

Even though some athletes compete because of their national pride, it can be suggested that nationalism is more established by the nations rather than by the athletes representing particular nations, because of their national awareness. According to this assumption, the debate of nationalism should perhaps be contextualised solely in a global sense, rather than in the context of individual athletes.

> It's an interesting idea in an increasingly globalized world – these athletes are switching to countries with better training opportunities, for the chance to become the strongest athlete possible. These athletes are competing in the Olympics to be the best in their sport, not for a love of country.IA (Davis, 2018)

Assuming that athletes are mainly focused on their careers, rather than their country, one consequence is an increasing industrialisation and economisation of the Olympics, as well as global sport in general. Regardless of the separation of Olympic athletes and other members of society, these different intentions might split the athlete community itself. On the one side are athletes that want to represent their nation with pride, and on the other side are athletes that are career driven. It needs to be mentioned that athletes can also switch nationality to represent the nationality they are proud of, but they switch because of better opportunities or because they are already related to the nation for which they want to compete. Between debates of citizenship, national belonging and representation, the economy and politics, industrialisation and materialisation, financial aspects, and simply competition in sport, it is hard to declare a common framework in which the debate on nationalism can take place. There are various approaches towards the discovery of the modern concept of nationalism in global sport. Previously in this chapter, as well as in other chapters, this Thesis has already referred to the dual and reciprocal existence of internationalism and national awareness. In general, nationalism and internationalism are understood as contrary. It can already be concluded that, on the one hand, nationalism cannot exist without internationalism and vice versa. On the other hand, the contexts of nationalism and internationalism often exclude one another. The concept of pan-nationalism already allows a parallel analysis of nationalism in a global context. Still, pan-nationalism is not a common way of analysing nationalism in international structures. The reason for this is that the concept is already attached to a particular conceptual framework. The term 'pan-nationalism' is mainly embedded in Eastern European contexts. Furthermore, pan-national approaches often focus on biological aspects of spreading nationalism. Moreover, different pan-national movements rarely accept each other. '*Pan-*' already refers to '*all-*', and nationalism still has an ideological character. Regardless of other critics of the concept of pan-nationalism, it can be suggested that the problem of pan-nationalism is that it is a supranational structure, applied to certain political movements. In the case of nationalism, it is a concept that can be used to explain particular national structures. However, the concept of pan-nationalism already suggests global transnational structures, but is still applied to certain movements which might exclude other pan-national movements. As assumed before, every problem in applying any form of nationalism theory emerges because a wide theoretical concept is attached to specific practical strings. In analysing migration in the context of the Olympics and nationalism, a wide concept of post-nationalism might be a more appropriate reference point. Post-nationalism is not particular understood as a concept, but more as a movement. Furthermore, does not occupy a contrary position to nationalism. Moreover, it is a modification of the concept of nationalism. A wide understanding of post-nationalism suggests an adaption of all altered forms of nationalism, so long as they refer to supranational structures. Asides from this point, post-nationalism takes the changing relation of national and international structures into account. Through a post-national understanding, people's identity is not bound to a nation-state, but rather to cross-national, supranational, and global identification. Moreover, contrary to some critics' views on some pan-national approaches, post-nationalism analysis does not necessarily consider the particular role of the nation-state. Therefore, in the case of migration, a wide post-national approach might be more appropriate to analyse modern global sport. Neither pan-nationalism, with its biological and territorial limits, nor internationalism, with its mainly entirely global approaches, seem to be eligible for an analysis of the Olympics and the migration of athletes. Furthermore, because post-nationalism does not necessarily refer to a specific concept, but rather to a process, it can be assumed that particular ideological understandings do not restrict the analysis. However, the prefix *'post-'* suggests in general that a previous 'movement' itself is over, but a modified 'movement' emerged from its legacy. Another example would be colonialism and post-colonialism. Some people claim that the prefix *'post-'* is not appropriate, because the original movement is not yet over. Therefore, this Bachelor Thesis does not explore if the prefix *'post-'* is legitimate. Moreover, in analysis, the term post-nationalism adapts a historical event that changed and therefore needs to be put into a modern context. Furthermore, this term is more convenient for the context of the Olympic Movement, where nationalism and internationalism co-exist.

The centre of this paper's analysis was the the debate over nationalism in context of the Olympics. According to this, this paper addressed whether the Olympics strengthen nationalism or if they promote international movement. The first part contained the introduction on different disciplines of migration research, as well as a particular consideration of international and transnational studies. With the introduction of the world-systems theory and human capital theory, an international analytical frame was constructed. Within this frame, the analysis of nationalism as a transnational movement could take place. Therefore, ideology was conceptualised as a phenomenon, of which nationalism is a sub-category. With the understanding of ideology as a belief system, the religious character of nationalism could be considered and be linked to the Olympic Games. In general, two analysing contexts can be determined: on the one hand, legal and practical definition, and on the other hand, constructed thoughts. An example of this would be the understanding of nation and state. While many theorists tend to define a state as a territorially limited area, a nation has no practical limits. It might be possible to define what a nation determines, but is hard to tie a nation to any fixed qualities. Another example would be the understanding of citizenship. In common understanding citizenship and national identity are often not adequately separated. The difficulties of establishing a general interpretation might be coherent, but it leads to falsifications of the analysis. As a conclusion of this paper, citizenship is defined as a legal status, noted in documents and connected to rights. Contrarily, national identity does not necessarily require a practical determination, but rather it is an individually constructed feeling, often related to heritage. In the context of diasporas, the debate of citizenship and national identity reaches its most intensive form. Regardless of whether the conceptual understanding of diaspora is more useful in the context of citizenship or national identity, the most interesting and important aspect is the transnational link. According to this, the existence of transnational communities requires a wide and extended concept of state and nation. As one conclusion of this Bachelor Thesis, ideology is a typical example of an analytical concept of constructed thoughts. The analysis of ideology has shown that it is not necessarily solely related to a certain worldview, but also to a political movement. On the one hand, with its character of a belief system ideology and religion can be seen as units of the same analysis. On the other hand, its political features enable an analytical relation to nationalism. In general, the aspect of politics only relates to congruent ideas and interests of people, and the aim of their achievements. Therefore, nationalism is more of a movement than a condition.

While the analysis of global and international structures, as well as the connection of religion, ideology and nationalism, constructed the theoretical framework of the analysis, the practical example of the Olympics focus point. Related to the human capital theory, the economic and political character of global modern sport, in the context of athletes as sporting capital, could be explored. In summary, the international capitalistic and industrial character of the Olympic Games extended enormously. Relevant examples of this phenomenon are the trading of foreign-born athletes and the increasing financial efforts of the Olympics. Furthermore, previous chapters explored the extreme differentiations between the historical origins of the modern Olympic Movement and the modern Games. Another conclusion of this Bachelor Thesis is that the IOC is a perfect example of how modern sport can be analysed within the world-systems theory. With the general results of the analysis and the theoretical background, the six central assumptions, as well as the general question of this Bachelor Thesis, can be answered and commented on.

The first assumption is that *In modern society, sport is only a tool of power division, with the Olympics as a practical example.* This assumption cannot be confirmed or refuted. The generalised assumption that sport is only a tool of power division is false. However, as can be summarised from the analysis, modern sport is a tool of global networking. Economic and political fields are strongly tied to modern sport. The Olympic Games, for example, are one of the most famous international sporting events across the globe. With the rankings of the athletes' performances and comparison of the national Olympic Teams, the nations' presentations can improve, but also deteriorate. Parallel to the image transformation of nations, through the participation at the Olympics, the number of investors can also increase and international networks can extend. Therefore, economics and politics of a nation are also influenced. As a result, the cross-national influence of a nation can increase or decrease as well. Hence, modern global sport, such as the Olympic Games, is a tool of power division, or at least of achieving a higher rank in the world-system. However, modern sport is not solely a tool of power division, as an be proved by the origins of the modern Olympics, as the Ancient Games highlighted class-society. Elite sport requires a certain physical education and this goes along with financial effort.

The second assumption of this paper was that *National awareness cannot be an important aspect of the Olympics, if nations trade with foreign-born athletes.* In common understanding, people might suggest that national thought has weakened due to the increasing number of foreign-born athletes. In summary, the opposite can actually be assumed. On the one hand, the nationality switching of athletes might split the athletic community. Some athletes compete in honour of their native country and others compete for countries that provide them with the best physical education or financial support. Another case that needs to be referred to is athletes that already had double citizenship, without changing nationality just for the Olympic Games. However, the increasing attention towards nationality switches could strengthen the national awareness of athletes that do not support nationality switches, as well as of spectators of the Olympic Games. As can be concluded from the analysis, the Olympic Games actually should construct an area in which elite athletes and team can compete again each other, without being a competition or ranking of nations. It could be suggested that the nationalistic character of the Olympic Games is mainly forced by nations in order to enable representation of their interests and their national character, which is then supported by the IOC to promote the Games. Thereby, the national awareness of each nation's people can strongly increase. As a final conclusion of this assumption, national awareness plays a big role in the Olympic Games, but more in the context of each nation and the spectators, rather than in the context of the individual athletes or teams.

The third assumption suggests that *Nationalism and Internationalism need to be separated in theory but they are co-existing in practice.* It is necessary to construct a theoretical understanding of nationalism and internationalism, but the analysis highlighted that they should not be separated completely in analysis. As can be summarised, they co-exist in theory, but merge in practice. Therefore, nationalism and internationalism should be analysed together. The separated understandings of both terms are traditional, but do not fit into modern society. As already assumed in the analysis, cross-national communities require a modification and fusion of both terms.

According to the fourth assumption of this Bachelor Thesis, *In times of double citizenship and diasporas, nationalism is getting weaker.* Through the outcomes of the analysis, this assumption can be refuted. First of all, it could already be summarised that the traditional form of nationalism does not fit into modern cross-national dynamics. Furthermore, diasporas themselves can be labelled as national movements. Since diasporas have no territorial limit, they especially depend on national identity and community. A diaspora can consist of more than just one group. In other words, the emergence of diasporas strengthens nationalism, rather than weakening it. In the context of double citizenship, the answer might be even simpler. Nationalism is neither weakened nor strengthened through double citizenship. According to the outcome of the analysis, double citizenship is only a legal status. Furthermore, this paper agrees with this definition of double citizenship, even if there are other approaches. Assuming that nationalism is a constructed thought, tied to national awareness, the legal status of citizenship does not affect nationalism. Moreover, it could be suggested that the existence of people with double citizenship affects the national awareness of people with single citizenship, especially for people who argue that everyone should just have one citizenship. In this case, one assumption would be that double citizenship strengthens nationalism and nationalism's awareness of people with single citizenship.

The fifth assumption that *The Olympics lost the connection to their religious roots and became a global promotion for each countries' identity.* can just be particular approved in the context of this Thesis. Even though the Olympic Games have become a global promotion for nations, they have not necessarily lost their religious roots. This has one simple reason. According to the IOC, the aim of the Olympics is to honour their ancient roots. As can be concluded from the analysis, Olympism is often analysed in a religious context. Although Olympism should not be understood as a religion in and of itself, its character is similar to traditional understandings of religious movements.

The central question of this paper was whether the Olympics strengthen nationalism or whether they promote the migration movement. This paper has argued that they do strengthen nationalism, but in a different way to traditional understandings. While the athletes are mainly not interested in which country they represent, spectators are even more interested in national representation. Nations use the Olympic Games to promote themselves and spectators are affected by that. Furthermore, the cross-national movement of athletes increases and therefore migration becomes more of a focus point. Especially since the establishment of the ROT, the debate of refugees and foreign-born athletes has extended. Moreover, the IOC used the ROT to promote the international network of the Olympic Movement. This might have been with good intentions, but it also can be criticised. Assuming that the ideological thought of promoting the refugee crisis, as the IOC mentioned itself, intends to positively affect the lives of refugees all over the world, it can be questioned why all the ROT's financial investment is not used to support other projects. In general, extravagant amounts of money are generated through the Olympic Games and also invested in them. It is a mass media spectacle to entertain spectators. Without the spectators/money, it is clear that the Olympics would not have achieved such high levels of success as they have. Finally, the Olympic Games promote the migration movement, but, as the analysis of this paper suggests, this might be more ineffective than successful.

Anon., 2015. SBS News: Foreign athletes to be fast-tracked. [Online]
Available at: https://www.sbs.com.au/news/foreign-athletes-to-be-fast-tracked
[Accessed 14 June 2020].

Anon., 2016. Fox Sports: America's best foreign imports in sports. [Online]
Available at: https://www.foxsports.com/mlb/gallery/foreign-imports-athletes-united-states-success-112012 [Accessed 14 June 2020].

Anon., 2016. Transfer Go: Migrant Olympic Game Winners. [Online]
Available at: https://www.transfergo.com/en/blog/migrant-olympic-game-winners/
[Accessed 14 June 2020].

Anon., 2018. Global Mobility Management: Can Olympic Athletes Change The Country They Represent?. [Online] Available at: https://info.caprelo.com/blog/can-olympic-athletes-change-the-country-they-represent [Accessed 11 June 2020].

Azzellini, D., 2011. Theorie-Wegweiser (Teil 1) : Nation: Begriffsklärung und Darstellung verschiedener Analyseansätze. [Online] Available at: http://www.azzellini.net/sites/azzellini.net/files/Theorie-Wegweiser_Teil_1.pdf [Accessed 03 May 2020].

Bartram, D., Poros, M. V. & Monforte, P., 2014. Key Concepts in Migration. Los Angeles, USA; London, UK; New Delhi, IN; Singapore, SG; Washington D.C., USA: SAGE Publications.

Bean, F. D. & Brown, S. K., 2015. Demography Analyses of Immigration. In: C. B. Brettell & J. F. Hollifield, eds. Migration Theory. Talking Across Disciplines. 3rd edition. New York, USA: Routledge, pp. 67-89.

Beissinger, M., 2000. Nationalisms that bark and nationalisms that bite: Ernest Gellner and the substantiation of nations. In: J. A. Hall, ed. The State of the Nation. Ernest Gellner and the Theory of Nationalism. New York, USA: Cambridge University Press, pp. 169-190.

Bockrath, F. & Forudastan, F., 2004. Internationalismus und Nationalismus bei den Olympischen Spielen. Interview mit Frank Bockrath, Professor für Sportwissenschaft an der Technischen Universität Darmstadt. [Online] Available at: https://www.deutschlandfunk.de/internationalismus-und-nationalismus-bei-den-olympischen.694.de.html?dram:article_id=61288[Accessed 14 June 2020].

Bosniak, L., 2006. The Citizen and the Alien : Dilemmas of Contemporary Membership, Princeton, USA; Oxford, UK: Princeton University Press, Available at: ProQuest Ebook Central [Accessed 19 April 2020].

Brenner, N., 2011. The Space of the World: Beyond State-Centrism?. In: B. Robbins, N. Tanoukhi & D. Palumbo-Liu, eds. Immanuel Wallerstein and the Problem of the World : System, Scale, Culture. Durham, UK: Duke University Press, Available at: ProQuest Ebook Central [Accessed 4 May 2020], pp. 101-137.

Brettell, C. B. & Hollifield, J. F., 2015. Migration Theory. Talking Across Disciplines. 3rd ed. New York, USA: Routledge.

Breuilly, J., 2005. Nationalism and the State. In: P. Spencer & H. Wollman, eds. Nations and Nationalsim. A Reader. Edinburgh, UK: Edinburgh University Press, Available at: ProQuest Ebook Central [Accessed 08 May 2020], pp. 61-73.

Brubaker, R., 2000. Myths and misconceptions in the study of nationalism. In: J. A. Hall, ed. The State of the Nation. Ernest Gellner and the Theory of Nationalism. New York, USA: Cambridge University Press, pp. 272-306.

Carpentier, F., 2018. Henri de Baillet-Latour: Globalising the Olympic Movement. In: E. Bayle & P. Clastres, eds. Global Sport Leaders: A Biographical Analysis of International Sport Management. Lausanne, CH: Palgrave Macmillan, Available at: ProQuest Ebook Centrala [Accessed 13 May 2020], pp. 107-123.

Castles, S., de Haas, H. & Miller, M. J., 2014. The Age of Migration. International Population Movements in the Modern World. 5th ed. Hampshire, UK: PALGRAVE MACMILLAN.

Chemi, E. & Fahey, M., 2016. How some Middle East countries are 'buying' Olympic medals. [Online] Available at: https://www.cnbc.com/2016/08/16/how-some-middle-east-countries-are-buying-olympic-medals.html [Accessed 6 June 2020].

Clastres, P., 2018. Pierre de Coubertin: The Inventor of the Olympic Tradition. In: E. Bayle & P. Clastres, eds. Global Sport Leaders : A Biographical Analysis of International Sport Management. Lausanne, CH: Palgrave Macmillan, Available at: ProQuest Ebook Central [Accessed 13 May 2020], pp. 33-60.

Clastres, P. & Bayle, E., 2018. Introduction: Becoming a Global Sport Leader. In: E. Bayle & P. Clastres, eds. Global Sport Leaders : A Biographical Analysis of International Sport Management. Lausanne, CH: Palgrave Macmillan, Available at: ProQuest Ebook Central [Accessed 13 May 2020], pp. 1-30.

Danielsson, S., 2011. Pan-nationalism reframed: nationalism, 'diaspora', the role of the 'nation-state' and the global age. In: D. Halikiopoulou & S. Vasilopoulou, eds. Nationalism and Globalisation : Conflicting or Complementary?. New York, USA: Taylor & Francis Group, Available at: ProQuest Ebook Central [Accessed 11 May 2020], pp. 41-61.

Davis, M., 2018. CAN WE HAVE THE OLYMPICS WITHOUT NATIONALISM?. [Online] Available at: http://bullandbearmcgill.com/can-olympics-without-nationalism/ [Accessed 14 June 2020].

Dormal, M., 2017. Nation und Repräsentation. Theorie, Geschichte und Gegenwart eines umstrittenen Verhältnisses. 1st ed. Baden-Baden, DE: Nomos Verlagsgesellschaft.

Durkheim, E., 2016. The Elementary Forms of the Religious Life. Dinslaken, DE: anboco, Available at: ProQuest Ebook Central [Accessed 20 April 2020].

Fahey, M., 2016. CNBC. Qatar and Bahrain aren't the only countries boosted by foreign-born Olympians. [Online] Available at: https://www.cnbc.com/2016/08/18/qatar-and-bahrain-are-not-the-only-countries-boosted-by-foreign-born-olympians.html [Accessed 11 June 2020].

Faist, T., Fauser, M. & Reisenauer, E., 2014. Das Transnationale in der Migration. Eine Einführung. Weinheim, DE; Basel, DE: Beltz Juventa.

Faulks, K., 2000. Citizenship. 1st ed. London, UK: Routledge Taylor & Francis Group, Available at: ProQuest Ebook Central [Accessed 12 May 2020].

Favell, A., 2001. Philosophies of Integration. Immigration and the idea of Citizenship in France and Britain. 2nd ed. Hampshire, UK: PALGRAVE.

Favell, A., 2015. Migration Theory Rebooted? Asymmetric Challenges in a Global Agenda. In: C. B. Brettell & J. F. Hollifield, eds. Migration Theory. Talking Across Disciplines. 3rd edition. New York, USA: Routledge, pp. 318-328.

FitzGerald, D. S., 2015. The Sociology of International Migration. In: C. B. Brettell & J. F. Hollifield, eds. Migration Theory. Talking Across Disciplines. 3rd edition. New York, USA: Routledge, pp. 115-147.

Fix, B., 2018. The Trouble With Human Capital Theory. In: Real-World Economics Review. Bristol, UK: Worl Economics Association, Available at: http://bnarchives.yorku.ca/568/ [Accessed 01 May 2020], pp. 15-32.

Flyvbjerg, B., Stewart, A. & Budzier, A., 2017. The Oxford Olympics Study 2016: Cost and Cost Overrun, Oxford: Saïd Business School, Available at: https://eureka.sbs.ox.ac.uk/6195/1/2016-20.pdf [Accessed 11 June 2020].

Friedman, G., 2016. Nationalism, technology, and the Olympics. [Online] Available at: https://www.euractiv.com/section/global-europe/opinion/nationalism-technology-and-the-olympics/ [Accessed 14 June 2020].

Gabaccia, D. R., 2015. Time and Temporality in Migration Studies. In: C. B. Brettell & J. F. Hollifield, eds. Migration Theory. Talking Across Disciplines. 3rd edition. New York, USA: Routledge, pp. 37-66.

Geertz, C., 1973. The Interpretation of Cultures. Selected Essays by Clifford Geertz. New York, USA: Basic Books, Inc., Publishers.

Gellner, E., 2000. The State of the Nation. Ernest Gellner and the Theory of Nationalism. 3rd ed. New York, USA: Cambridge University Press.

Gellner, E., 2005. Nationalism and Modernity. In: P. Spencer & H. Wollman, eds. Nations and Nationalism. A Reader. Edinburgh, UK: Edinburgh Universitiy Press, Available at: ProQuest Ebook Central [Accessed 08 May 2020], pp. 40-47.

Goldin, C., 2014. Human Capital. In: C. Diebolt & M. Haupert, eds. Handbook of Cliometrics. Department of Economics Harvard University and National Bureau of Economic Research: Springer Verlag, Available at: https://scholar.harvard.edu/files/goldin/files/human_capital_handbook_of_cliometrics_0.pdf [Access 01 May 2020].

Gough, C., 2020. Number of participating countries in the Summer Olympics from 1896 to 2016. [Online] Available at: https://www.statista.com/statistics/280462/summer-olympics-1896-2012-number-of-participating-countries/ [Accessed 11 June 2020].

Gough, C., 2020. Total Olympic Games marketing revenues from 1993 to 2016(in million U.S. dollars). [Online] Available at: https://www.statista.com/statistics/274453/marketing-revenues-of-olympic-games-in-total-since-1993/ [Accessed 11 June 2020].

Guttmann, A., 2020. Olympic Winter Games - partners in the OCOGs domestic sponsorship programs 2018. [Online] Available at: https://www.statista.com/statistics/199438/ocogs-sponsor-programme-partners-for-the-winter-games-since-1998/ [Accessed 11 June 2020].

Halikiopoulou, C. & Vasilopoulou, S., 2011. Introduction: bridging the gap between nationalism and globalisation. In: D. Halikiopoulou & S. Vasilopoulou, eds. Nationalism and Globalisation : Conflicting or Complementary?. New York, USA: Taylor & Francis Group, Available at: ProQuest Ebook Central [Accessed 11 May 2020], pp. 1-13.

Hall, J. A., 2011. Nationalism might change its character, again. In: D. Halikiopoulou & S. Vasilopoulou, eds. Nationalism and Globalisation : Conflicting or Complementary?. New York, USA: Taylor & Francis Group, Available at: ProQuest Ebook Central [Accessed 11 May 2020], pp. 17-26.

Harris, E., 2009. Nationalism. Edinburgh, UK: Edinburgh University Press, Available at: ProQuest Ebook Central [Accessed 11 May 2020].

Hartog, J. & Maassen van den Brink, H., 2007. Human Capital : Advances in Theory and Evidence. New York, USA: Cambridge University Press, Available at: ProQuest Ebook Central [Accessed 28 April 2020].

Herzmann, H., 2014. Nationale Identität : Mythos und Wirklichkeit am Beispiel Österreichs. Hamburg, DE: tredition, Available at: ProQuest Ebook Central [Accessed 11 May 2020].

Hollifield, J. F. & Wong, T. K., 2015. The Politics of International Migration. How Can We "Bring The State Back In"?. In: C. B. Brettell & J. F. Hollifield, eds. Migration Theory. Talking Across Disciplines. 3rd edition. New York, USA: Routledge, pp. 227-288.

Hroch, M., 2000. Real and constructed: the nature of the nation. In: J. A. Hall, ed. The State of the Nation. Ernest Gellner and the Theory of Nationalism. New York, USA: Cambridge University Press, pp. 91-106.

Hutchinson, J., 2011. Globalisation and nation formation in the longue durée . In: D. Halikiopoulou & S. Vasilopoulou, eds. Nationalism and Globalisation : Conflicting or Complementary?. New York, USA: Taylor & Francis Group, Available at: ProQuest Ebook Central [Accessed 11 May 2020], pp. 84-99.

IOC, 2016. REFUGEE OLYMPIC TEAM TO SHINE SPOTLIGHT ON WORLD-WIDE REFUGEE CRISIS. [Online] Available at: https://www.olympic.org/news/refugee-olympic-team-to-shine-spotlight-on-worldwide-refugee-crisis [Accessed 16 June 2020].

IOC, 2019. Olympic Charter. [Online] Available at: https://stillmed.olympic.org/media/Document%20Library/OlympicOrg/General/EN-Olympic-Charter.pdf [Accessed 15 June 2020].

Jakab, É., 2014. Sponsoren und Athleten im römischen Recht: Das ‚Ausbildungsdarlehen‘ der Athleten?. In: K. Harter-Uibopuu & T. Kruse, eds. Sport und Recht in der Antike. Beiträge zum 2. Wiener Kolloquium zur Antiken Rechtsgeschichte 27.-28.10.2011. Wien, DE: Verlag Holzhausen GmbH, https://roemr.univie.ac.at/fileadmin/user_upload/i_roemisches_recht/Publikationen/Gamauf_Pro_virtute_certamen.pdf [Accessed 17 May 2020], pp. 249-273.

Jansen, J. & Engbersen, G., 2017. Have the Olympic Games become more migratory? A comparative historical perspective. [Online] Available at: file:///C:/Users/maria_zzyqni0/Downloads/Research_paper.pdf [Accessed 10 June 2020].

Jansen, J., Oonk, G. & Engbersen, G., 2018. Nationality swapping in the Olympic field: towards the marketization of citizenship? In: Citizenship Studies. 22nd vol., 5th ed. 523-539: Routledge, https://www.tandfonline.com/doi/pdf/10.1080/13621025.2018.1477921?needAccess=true.

Jirásek, I., 2015. Religion, Spirituality, and Sport: From Religio Athletae Toward Spiritus Athletae. [Online] Available at: https://doi.org/10.1080/00336297.2015.1048373 [Accessed 17 May 2020].

Klotz, A., 2013. Migration and National Identity in South Africa, 1860–2010. New York, USA: Cambridge University Press, Available at: ProQuest Ebook Central [Accessed 18 April 2020].

Knott, K., 2011. Moving People Changing Places. Sport, Ethnicity, Migration. [Online] Available at: http://www.movingpeoplechangingplaces.org/identities-cultures/sporting-diasporas.html [Accessed 11 June 2020].

Koslowski, R., 2001. Demographic Boundary Maintenance in World Politics: Of International Norms on Dual Nationality. In: M. Albert, D. Jacobson & Y. Lapid, eds. Identities, Borders, Orders : Rethinking International Relations Theory. Minneapolis, USA: University of Minnesota Press, Available at: ProQuest Ebook Central [Accessed 12 May 2020], pp. 203-223.

Kukuk, M., 2015. Spitzensport und Migration. Theoretische Überlegungnen zu Lebensmittelpunktverzetzungen von Spitzensportlern (unpublished dissertation, faculty of natural sciences). [Online] Available at: https://core.ac.uk/reader/50521649 [Accessed 17 May 2020].

Kunze, R., 2007. Nation und Nationalismus. A. Bauerkämper, P. Steinbach & E. Wolfrum, eds. Darmstadt, DE: wbg Academic, Available at: ProQuest Ebook Central [Accessed 11 May 2020].

Lee, R. E., 2011. The Modern World-System: Its Structures, Its Geoclutures, Its Crisis and Transformation. In: B. Robbins, N. Tanoukhi & D. Palumbo-Liu, eds. Immanuel Wallerstein and the Problem of the World: System, Scale, Culture. Durham, UK: Duke Universitiy Press, Available at: ProQuest Ebook Central [Accessed 4 May 2020], pp. 27-40.

Máiz, R., 2011. The Inner Frontier : The Place of Nation in the Political Theory of Democracy and Federalism. Brussels, BE: P.I.E. Peter Lang, Available at: ProQuest Ebook Central [Accessed 11 May 2020].

Mallon, B., Heijmans, J. & Evans, H., 2017. OLYMPIAN IMMIGRANTS. [Online] Available at: https://olympstats.com/2017/02/20/olympian-immigrants/ [Accessed 10 June 2020].

Mann, M., 2005. Has Globalisation ended the Rise and Rise of the Nation-State?. In: P. Spencer & H. Wollman, eds. Nations and Nationalism. A Reader. Edinburgh, UK: Edinburgh University Press, Available at: ProQuest Ebook Central [Accessed 08 May 2020], pp. 279-300.

Martínez Vela, C. A., 2001. World Systems Theory. [Online] Available at: http://web.mit.edu/esd.83/www/notebook/WorldSystem.pdf [Accessed 01 May 2020].

Martins, H., 2014. Time and theory in sociology. In: J. Rex, ed. Approaches to Sociology (RLE Social Theory) : An Introduction to Major Trends in British Sociology,. Florence, IT: Taylor & Francis Group, Available at: ProQuest Ebook Central [Accessed 20 April 2020], pp. 246-294.

McBride, J., 2018. The Economics of Hosting the Olympic Games. [Online] Available at: https://www.cfr.org/backgrounder/economics-hosting-olympic-games [Accessed 11 June 2020].

Miah, A. & Garcia, B., 2012. The Olympics: the Basics. London, UK: Taylor & Francis Group, Available at: ProQuest Ebook Central [Accessed 17 May 2020].

Morris, W. F., 2009. Understanding Ideology. Lanham, USA: University Press of America, Available at: ProQuest Ebook Central [Accessed 13 May 2020].

Mouzelis, N., 2000. Ernest Gellner's theory of nationalism: some definitional and methodological issues. In: J. A. Hall, ed. The State of the Nation. Ernest Gellner and the Theory of Nationalism. New York, USA: Cambridge University Press, pp. 158-165.

Nowrasteh, A., 2016. Immigrant Olympians. [Online] Available at: https://www.cato.org/blog/immigrant-olympians [Accessed 11 June 2020].

Olaniyan, D. A. & Okemakinde, T., 2008. Human Capital Theory: Implications for Educational Development. In: Pakistan Journal of Social Sciences 5. Ibadan, NG: Department of Educational Management University of Ibadan, Available at: http://docsdrive.com/pdfs/medwelljournals/pjssci/2008/479-483.pdf [Accessed 01 May 2020], pp. 479-483.

O'Leary, B., 2000. Ernest Gellner's diagnoses of nationalism: a critical overview, or, what is living and what is dead in Ernest Gellner's philosophy of nationalism? In: J. A. Hall, ed. The State of the Nation. Ernest Gellner and the Theory of Nationalism. New York, USA: Cambridge University Press, pp. 40-88.

Orwell, G., 2020. Über Nationalismus. München: dtv Verlagsgesellschaft mbH und Co. KG.

Oxford Dictionary, human capital. Oxford Learner's Dictionaries. [Online] Available at: https://www.oxfordlearnersdictionaries.com/definition/english/human-capital?q=Human+Capital [Accessed 01 May 2020].

Parry, J. & Girginov, V., 2005. The Olympic Games Explained: A Student Guide to the Evolution of the Modern Olympic Games. London, UK: Taylor & Francis Group, Available at: ProQuest Ebook Central [18 May 2020].

Pritchard, D. M., 2012. Sport, Democracy and War in Classical Athens. New York, USA: Cambridge University Press, Available at: ProQuest Ebook Central [Accessed 17 May 2020].

Provan, A., 2011. The Work of Sport in the Age of International Acquisition. How Arabized Kenyan runners have brought glory to the Emirates and undermined the patriotic conceit of the international-sports economy. [Online] Available at: https://bidoun.org/articles/the-work-of-sport-in-the-age-of-international-acquisition [Accessed 14 June 2020].

Reid, L. H., 2017. Why Olympia Matters for Modern Sport Warren Fraleigh Distinguished. In: L. H. Reid & E. Moore, eds. Reflecting on Modern Sport in Ancient Olympia Book Subtitle: Proceedings of the 2016 Meeting of the International Association for the Philosophy of Sport at the International Olympic Academy. s.l.:Parnassos Press – Fonte Aretusa, Available at: https://www.jstor.org/stable/j.ctvbj7gdq.18 [Accessed 17 May 2020], pp. 171-188.

Reznik, J., 2017. The Essence of Sport. In: H. L. Reid & E. Moore, eds. Reflecting on Modern Sport in Ancient Olympia. Proceedings of the 2016 Meeting of the International Association for the Philosophy of Sport at the International Olympic Academy. s.l.:Parnassos Press – Fonte Aretusa, Available at: https://www.jstor.org/stable/j.ctvbj7gdq.12 [Accessed 17 May 2020], pp. 95-104.

Rowe, N. R., 2017. Sporting Capital: Transforming Sports Development Policy and Practice. London, UK; New York, USA: Taylor & Francis Group, Available at: ProQuest Ebook Central [Accessed 17 May 2020].

Smith, A., 2005. Ethno-Symbolism and the Study of Nationalism. In: P. Spencer & H. Wollman, eds. Nations and Nationalism. A Reader. Edinburgh, UK: Edinburgh University Press, Available at: ProQuest Ebook Central [Accessed 08 May 2020], pp. 23-31.

Smith, P. & Riley, A., 2009. cultural theory. an introduction. 2nd ed. Malden, USA; Oxford, UK: Blackwell Publishing.

Spencer, P. & Wollman, H., 2005. Good and Bad Nationalisms. In: P. Spencer & H. Wollman, eds. Nations and Nationalism. A Reader. Edinburgh, UK: Edinburgh University Press, Available at: ProQuest Ebook Central [Accessed 08 May 2020], pp. 197-217.

Stetter, S., 2007. Territorial Conflicts in World Society : Modern Systems Theory, International Relations and Conflict Studies. London, UK; New York, USA: Routledge Taylor & Francis Group, Available at: ProQuest Ebook Central [Accessed 28 April 2020].

Szporluk, R., 2000. Thoughts about change: Ernest Gellner and the history of nationalism. In: J. A. Hall, ed. The State of the Nation. Ernest Gellner and the Theory of Nationalism. New York, USA: Cambridge University Press, pp. 23-39.

Taylor, C., 2000. Nationalsim and modernity. In: J. A. Hall, ed. The State of the Nation. Ernest Gellner and the Theory of Nationalism. New York, USA: Cambridge University Press, pp. 191-218.

Thompson, K., 2015. World Systems Theory. [Online] Available at: https://revisesociology.com/2015/12/05/world-systems-theory/ [Accessed 01 May 2020].

Vasilogambros, M., 2016. Why Some Olympians Compete Against Their Home Country. Is switching nationalities just to compete in the games in the Olympic spirit?. [Online] Available at: https://www.theatlantic.com/news/archive/2016/08/why-some-olympians-compete-against-their-home-country/494648/ [Accessed 14 June 2020].

Waldinger, R. & Lichter, M. I., 2003. How the Other Half Works : Immigration and the Social Organization of Labor. London, UK; Berkeley/Los Angeles, USA: University of California Press, Available at: ProQuest Ebook Central [Accessed 19 April 2020].

Wallerstein, I., 1996. Historical Capitalism with Capitalist Civilization. 8th ed. London, UK; New York, USA: Verso, Available at: https://libcom.org/files/immanuel-wallerstein-historical-capitalism.pdf [Accessed 18 April 2020].

Wallerstein, I., 2007. World-Systems Analysis: An Introduction. 5th ed. Durham, UK: Duke University Press, Available at: ProQuest Ebook Central [Accessed 4 May 2020].

Wallerstein, I., 2013. World-system analysis, Yale University, USA: sociopedia.isa, Available at: http://www.sagepub.net/isa/resources/pdf/World-Systems%20analysis.pdf [Accessed 01 May 2020].

Weber, M., 1987. Max Weber: Economy and Society. An Outline of Interpretive Sociology. Roth, G./Wittich, C. eds.; 2nd ed. London, UK; Berkeley/Los Angeles, USA: University of California Press, Available at: https://archive.org/details/MaxWeberEconomyAndSociety/page/n1/mode/2up [Accessed 20 April 2020].

Wehler, H., 2016. Nationalismus : Geschichte, Formen, Folgen. 4th ed. München, DE: C.H. Beck, Available at: ProQuest Ebook Central [Accessed 11 May 2020].

Weliver, D., 2019. How Much Do Olympic (Both Summer And Winter) Athletes Earn?. [Online] Available at: https://www.moneyunder30.com/how-much-do-olympic-athletes-earn [Accessed 11 June 2020].

Wiggins, B., 2018. Why some Olympians can compete for countries they are not from. [Online] Available at: https://www.businessinsider.com/why-some-olympic-athletes-have-competed-for-multiple-countries-2018-2?r=DE&IR=T [Accessed 14 June 2020].

Wilson, D. & Lehren, W., 2008. The New York Times. Swapping Passports in Pursuit of Olympic Medals. [Online] Available at: https://www.nytimes.com/2008/06/15/sports/olympics/15citizen.html [Accessed 11 June 2020].

A: Tables

1. (%) foreign-born athletes by Olympic Team (1948-2012)

2. Diversity (D) among foreign-born athletes

3. Cross-continental movements of foreign-born Olympic athletes (1960)

4. Cross-continental movements of foreign-born Olympic athletes (2012)

5. Countries with the highest percentage of IA of OPB, since 1896

6. Countries that sent the most Olympians to compete for other nations

7. Most common combinations of receiving and origin countries of migrant athletes

8. Examples of Medal Bonus for Olympic Athletes (2018)

9. Sports-related cost overruns, Olympics 1960-2016; calculated in local currencies, real terms

10. Top three countries of using foregin-born athletes and losing native athletes (2018 Winter Olympic Games, Pyeongchang, South Korea)

11. Olympic Teams composed entirely of IA (2018 Winter Olympic Games, Pyeongchang, South Korea)

B. Figures

1. Number of partners in the OCOGs sponsorship programs for the Winter Games from 1998 to 2018

2. Total Olympic Games marketing revenues from 1993 to 2016 (in millions and U.S. dollars)

3. Foreign Born as a Percentage of Each U.S. Team

4. Broadcast Revenue from Olympic Television Rights Fees

5. Number of participating countries in the Summer Olympics from 1896 to 2016

6. Olympic nationality switches 1948 – 2016

A: Tables

Table 1: (%) foreign-born athletes by Olympic Teams (1948-2012)

	ARG	AUS	BRA	CAN	FRA	GBR	ITA	NLD	SPA	SWE	USA	TOT	UNK
1948	3.5%	2.7%	0.0%	5.5%	5.7%	10.2%	6.5%	10.7%	1.5%	1.7%	7.0%	6.2%	21.0%
1952	7.3%	1.2%	0.0%	4.7%	6.9%	4.3%	2.6%	14.4%	0.0%	1.5%	5.9%	4.8%	19.6%
1956	3.6%	6.5%	0.0%	4.3%	9.5%	5.3%	3.9%			4.5%	7.4%	6.0%	22.4%
1960	3.3%	11.6%	4.2%	18.8%	13.0%	8.3%	2.9%	8.2%	0.7%	4.5%	3.8%	6.9%	0.6%
1964	0.0%	7.9%	3.3%	13.9%	6.5%	5.9%	5.4%	7.2%	0.0%	1.1%	5.5%	5.8%	18.7%
1968	3.4%	6.3%	3.9%	23.7%	7.5%	8.4%	2.4%	6.5%	1.6%	5.0%	3.9%	6.6%	1.9%
1972	0.0%	5.4%	2.5%	20.7%	4.0%	6.0%	2.2%	7.6%	4.1%	4.6%	6.3%	6.3%	21.2%
1976	0.0%	5.0%	0.0%	19.5%	3.9%	9.5%	1.9%	4.6%	1.8%	5.2%	4.5%	7.1%	21.1%
1980	0.0%	5.8%	0.9%		6.6%	9.1%	1.3%	4.0%	2.6%	4.1%		4.3%	30.7%
1984		2.1%	0.0%	16.2%	4.6%	9.2%	2.6%	2.9%	0.6%	4.0%	6.1%	6.2%	13.0%
1988	0.8%	6.0%	0.0%	21.6%	6.0%	5.5%	2.4%	4.1%	3.9%	3.8%	4.4%	6.2%	12.8%
1992	1.2%	7.9%	1.1%	19.3%	8.8%	7.3%	3.0%	6.5%	3.3%	4.8%	5.3%	6.6%	7.8%
1996	0.6%	10.1%	1.8%	15.8%	8.6%	5.7%	2.9%	6.7%	5.9%	3.4%	6.3%	6.7%	3.8%
2000	2.1%	13.9%	1.0%	17.0%	8.0%	4.8%	8.0%	8.2%	5.3%	2.7%	5.3%	8.0%	1.5%
2004	1.3%	10.2%	2.1%	12.5%	11.4%	5.3%	10.7%	12.4%	5.7%	7.0%	5.4%	7.9%	0.0%
2008	2.3%	9.7%	1.1%	13.9%	7.1%	8.2%	7.2%	11.0%	8.5%	5.7%	6.1%	7.7%	0.0%
2012	2.9%	11.1%	2.0%	12.8%	9.3%	13.0%	8.5%	11.0%	10.1%	3.0%	8.1%	9.2%	0.0%

Source: Jansen & Engbersen, 2017, p. 6

Table 2: Diversity (D) among foreign-born athletes

	1960	2012
Argentina	0.444	0.625
Australia	0.860	0.935
Brazil	0.667	0.560
Canada	0.898	0.924
France	0.730	0.911
Great Britain	0.898	0.949
Italy	0.688	0.906
Netherlands	0.494	0.892
Spain (In 1960, only one athlete competing for Spain was born abroad, hence the outcome of zero diversity.)	0.000	0.923
Sweden	0.667	0.750
United States	0.860	0.962
All 11 countries	0.953	0.972

Source: Jansen & Engbersen, 2017, p. 9

Table 3: Cross-continental movements of foreign-born Olympic athletes (1960)

1960	Destination continent				
Origin continent	Europe	North America	Oceania	South America	Total
Africa	37.0%	0.0%	0.0%	0.0%	21.1%
Asia	19.2%	7.4%	27.3%	0.0%	17.2%
Europe	35.6%	85.2%	72.7%	83.3%	54.7%
North America	8.2%	3.7%	0.0%	0.0%	5.5%
Oceania	0.0%	3.7%	0.0%	0.0%	0.8%
South America	0.0%	0.0%	0.0%	16.7%	0.8%

Source: Jansen & Engbersen, 2017, p. 10

Table 4: Cross-continental movements of foreign-born Olympic athletes (2012)

2012	Destination continent				
Origin continent	Europe	North America	Oceania	South America	Total
Africa	26.0%	10.7%	26.7%	0.0%	21.5%
Asia	8.7%	16.0%	26.7%	22.2%	13.6%
Europe	35.8%	38.7%	35.6%	44.4%	36.8%
North America	20.8%	26.7%	8.9%	33.3%	20.9%
Oceania	2.3%	2.7%	2.2%	0.0%	2.3%
South America	6.4%	5.3%	0.0%	0.0%	5.0%

Source: Jansen & Engbersen, 2017, p. 11

Table 5: Countries with the highest percentage of IA of OPB/POB, since 1896

NOC	IA	#POB	%IA
Qatar	39	96	40.6%
Israel	110	281	39.1%
Ireland	138	634	21.8%
Liechtenstein	23	110	20.9%
Azerbaijan	25	126	19.8%
Canada	637	3978	16.0%
Cyprus	14	96	14.6%
Greece	213	1467	14.5%
New Zealand	145	1066	13.6%
Hong Kong	35	264	13.3%

Source: Mallon, et al., 2017

Table 6: Countries that sent the most Olympians to compete for other nations

COB	IA	#OPB	%IA
Georgia	38	112	33.9%
Serbia	40	126	31.7%
Jamaica	78	287	27.2%
Czech Republic (Czechia)	122	518	23.6%
Ethiopia	41	186	22.0%
Côte d'Ivoire	21	102	20.6%
Malaysia	50	246	20.3%
Trinidad & Tobago	23	137	16.8%
Kenya	66	405	16.3%
Morocco	59	379	15.6%

Source: Mallon, et al., 2017

Table 7: Most common combinations of receiving and origins countries of migrant athletes

COMPETED FOR	BORN IN	#COMBOS	%POSSIBLE
Canada	Jamaica	45	57.7%
United States	Norway	35	50.0%
Greece	Georgia	19	50.0%
United States	Japan	14	42.4%
United States	Ireland	21	37.5%
United States	Mexico	9	33.3%
Turkey	Bulgaria	14	28.0%
Germany	Kazakhstan	9	27.3%
Bahrain	Ethiopia	11	26.8%
Canada	Norway	17	24.3%
Bahrain	Kenya	16	24.2%

Source: Mallon, et al., 2017

Table 8: Examples of Medal Bonus for Olympic Athletes (2018)

Country	Total Rank	Gold	Silver	Bronze
Singapore	1	1,000,000 USD	500,000 USD	250,000 USD
Indonesia	2	746,000 USD	378,000 USD	188,000 USD
Kazakhstan	3	250,000 USD	150,000 USD	75,000 USD
USA	9	37,500 USD	22,500 USD	15,000 USD
Germany	11	22,000 USD	17,000 USD	11,000 USD
Canada	12	15,000 USD	11,000 USD	8,000 USD

Source: scheme based on Weliver, 2019

Table 9: Sports-related cost overruns, Olympics 1960-2016; calculated in local currencies, real terms

Games	Country	Type	Cost overrun %
Montreal 1976	Canada	Summer	720
Barcelona 1992	Spain	Summer	266
Atlanta 1996	United States	Summer	151
Sydney 2000	Australia	Summer	90
Athens 2004	Greece	Summer	49
Beijing 2008	China	Summer	2
London 2012	United Kingdom	Summer	76
Rio 2016*	Brazil	Summer	51
Average	-	*Summer*	*176*
Median	-	*Summer*	*83*
Grenoble 1968	France	Winter	181
Lake Placid 1980	United States	Winter	324
Sarajevo 1984	Yugoslavia	Winter	118
Calgary 1988	Canada	Winter	65
Albertville 1992	France	Winter	137
Lillehammer 1994	Norway	Winter	277
Nagano 1998	Japan	Winter	56
Salt Lake City 2002	United States	Winter	24
Torino 2006	Italy	Winter	80
Vancouver 2010	Canada	Winter	13
Sochi 2014	Russia	Winter	289
Average	-	*Winter*	*142*
Median	-	*Winter*	*118*

Source: Flyvbjerg, et al., 2017, p. 12

Table 10: Top three countries of using foreign-born athletes and losing native athletes (2018 Winter Olympic Games, Pyeongchang, South Korea)

COUNTRIES	NUMBER
USING ATHLETES	
SOUTH KOREA	18
CANADA	13
GERMNAY	11
LOSING ATHLETES	37
U.S.A.	37
CANADA	21
RUSSIA	19

Source: scheme based on Anon., 2018

Table 11: Olympic Teams composed entirely of IA (2018 Winter Olympic Games, Pyeongchang, South Korea)

COUNTRY	NUMBER
PUERTO RICO	1
MALTA	1
ERITREA	1
TIMOR-LESTE	1
TONGA	1
BERMUDA	1
KOSOVO	1
AZERBAIJAN	1
MAROCCO	2
BOLIVIA	2
NIGERIA	4
THAILAND	4

Source: scheme based on (Anon., 2018)

B: Figures

Figure 1: Number of partners in the OCOGs sponsorship programs for the Winter Games from 1998 to 2018

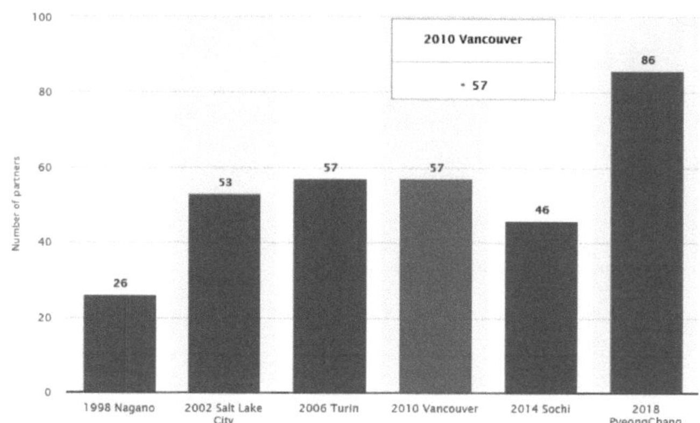

Source: Guttmann, 2020

Figure 2: Total Olympic Games marketing revenues from 1993 to 2016 (in millions and U.S. dollars)

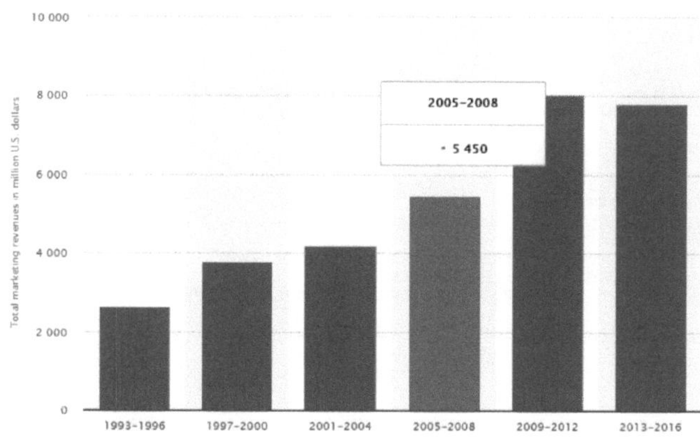

Source: Gough, 2020

Figure 3: Foreign Born as a Percentage of Each U.S. Team

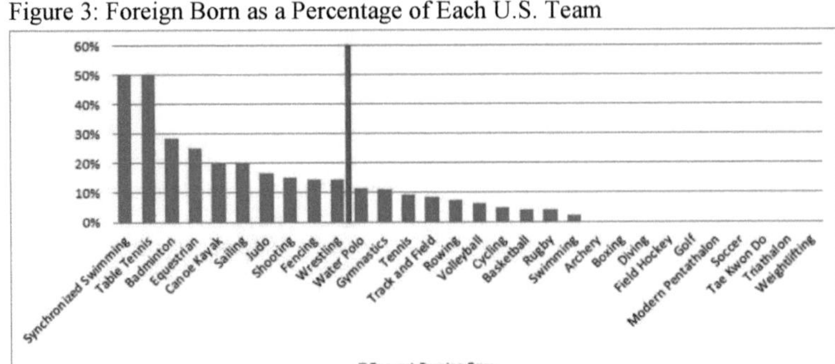

Source: Nowrasteh, 2016, based on data of *TeamUSA.org Sortable Roster*

Figure 4: Broadcast Revenue from Olympic Television Rights Fees

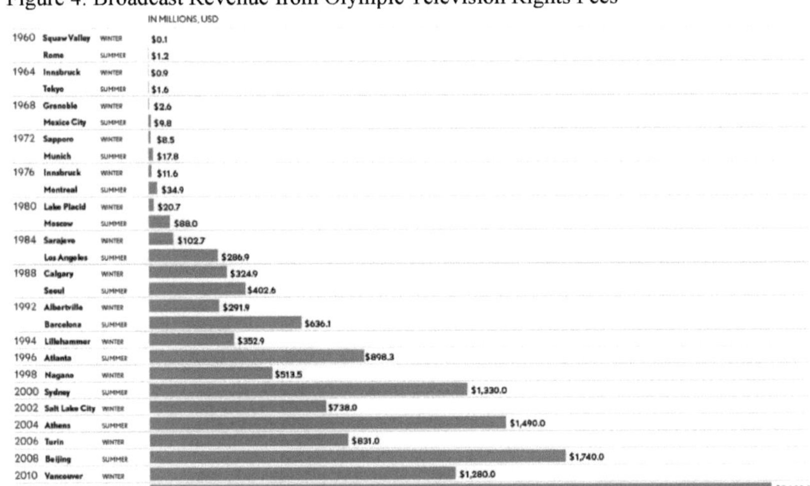

Year	City	Season	Revenue
1960	Squaw Valley	WINTER	$0.1
	Rome	SUMMER	$1.2
1964	Innsbruck	WINTER	$0.9
	Tokyo	SUMMER	$1.6
1968	Grenoble	WINTER	$2.6
	Mexico City	SUMMER	$9.8
1972	Sapporo	WINTER	$8.5
	Munich	SUMMER	$17.8
1976	Innsbruck	WINTER	$11.6
	Montreal	SUMMER	$34.9
1980	Lake Placid	WINTER	$20.7
	Moscow	SUMMER	$88.0
1984	Sarajevo	WINTER	$102.7
	Los Angeles	SUMMER	$286.9
1988	Calgary	WINTER	$324.9
	Seoul	SUMMER	$402.6
1992	Albertville	WINTER	$291.9
	Barcelona	SUMMER	$636.1
1994	Lillehammer	WINTER	$352.9
1996	Atlanta	SUMMER	$898.3
1998	Nagano	WINTER	$513.5
2000	Sydney	SUMMER	$1,330.0
2002	Salt Lake City	WINTER	$738.0
2004	Athens	SUMMER	$1,490.0
2006	Turin	WINTER	$831.0
2008	Beijing	SUMMER	$1,740.0
2010	Vancouver	WINTER	$1,280.0
2012	London	SUMMER	$2,600.0

Source: McBride, 2018

Figure 5: Number of participating countries in the Summer Olympics from 1896 to 2016

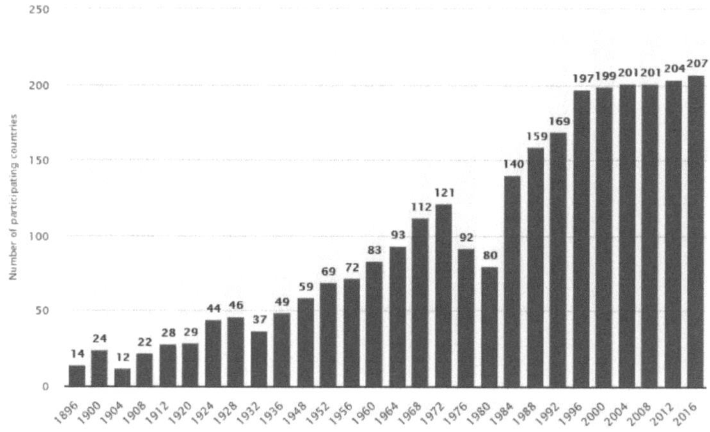

Source: Gough, 2020

Figure 6: Olympic nationality switches 1948 – 2016

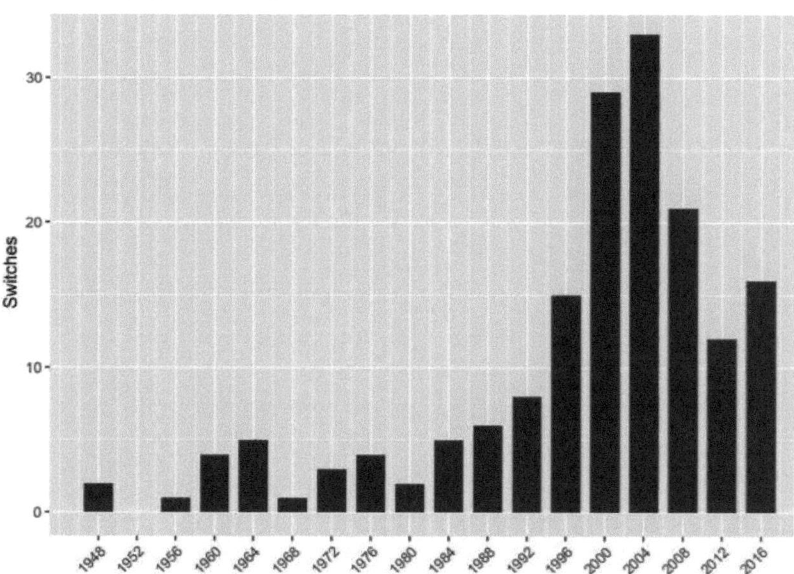

Source: (Jansen, et al., 2018, p. 530)